THE KENTUCKY DERBY

RUN FOR THE ROSES

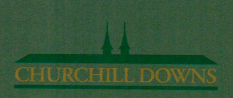

CHURCHILL DOWNS

A TEHABI BOOK

The Starting Gate
Derby Day, Twenty Minutes to Post

The starting gate stands empty, ready for another field of Derby horses to be loaded into the gate. As each goes in, the stall doors will be shut around them, and they will stand—nervous and excited, but poised to run for the roses.

Ahead, past the ancient Twin Spires of Churchill Downs, lies a one-quarter-mile straightaway. By the time the field has circled the track and returned to this spot, the gate will be pulled away, and the final quarter-mile stretch run to immortality will remain.

T

he hooves of a racehorse spend very little time on the ground. Dirt is kicked back from a horse's hooves as they catch the track and propel the thoroughbred forward. In full flight, top thoroughbred racehorses travel at speeds approaching 40 miles per hour.

W
PAST THE STANDS
DERBY DAY, THEN AND NOW

hether cheering

from a third-floor box seat, right, or crowding

the grounds in the 1926 Derby, below, fans

have come by the thousands for the

running of the Kentucky Derby every year

since 1875.

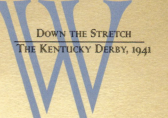

Whirlaway, ridden by famed jockey Eddie Arcaro, flies to an eight-length victory in the 1941 Derby, setting a track record of 2:01 2/5 that stood for twenty-one years.

SILVER CHARM

6

S AT THE WIRE
THE KENTUCKY DERBY, 1997

ilver Charm, the gun-metal gray, tenaciously holds off the furious late challenge of Captain Bodgit to triumph in the 1997 Kentucky Derby. Trained by Bob Baffert for owners Bob and Beverly Lewis, Silver Charm also won the Preakness Stakes in a photo finish, but lost a close one in the Belmont to just miss becoming a Triple Crown Champion. Later, Silver Charm was shipped halfway around the world to win the $4 Million Dubai World Cup.

THE KENTUCKY DERBY

RUN FOR THE ROSES

BY BILL DOOLITTLE

FOREWORD BY WALTER CRONKITE

TIME
LIFE
BOOKS

A TEHABI BOOK

W hat other event packs such long anticipation into such a swift climax? The Kentucky Derby offers just two minutes to decide the dreams of a lifetime.

Past the stands for the first time, jockeys vie for position in a field of nineteen horses in the 1995 Kentucky Derby. Eventual winner Thunder Gulch (far left, with white blinker mask) broke from an outside No. 16 post position, but jockey Gary Stevens had the colt on the move early to secure a forward placing, just behind the early pacesetters.

CHURCHILL DOWNS

ACKNOWLEDGMENTS

I wish to express my appreciation to Bill Doolittle Sr., the late Muriel Doolittle, and all our family; and to Bill Croley, Amy Roll, and all my loyal friends. I would also like to thank Leonard Lusky, Connie Barlow, Jack Barry, and Ross Eberman for their special contributions—as well as all the people at Tehabi Books and Churchill Downs, and everyone who hopes for the very best for the Kentucky Derby.

—BILL DOOLITTLE, LOUISVILLE, KENTUCKY

TEHABI BOOKS

Del Mar, California, www.tehabi.com

Nancy Cash
Managing Editor

Sarah Morgans
Developmental Editor

Allison Palmer
Copy Editor

Jeff Campbell
Copy Proofer

Ken DellaPenta
Indexer

Andy Lewis
Art Director

Kevin Giontzeneli
Assistant Art Director

Tom Lewis
Editorial and Design Director

Sam Lewis
Webmaster

Tim Connolly
Sales and Marketing Manager

Ross Eberman
Director of Custom Publishing

Maria Medina
Administrative Assistant

Sharon Lewis
Controller

Chris Capen
President

For more information on *The Kentucky Derby: Run for the Roses*, including corporate customized editions, please contact: Tehabi Books, 1201 Camino Del Mar, Suite 100, Del Mar, CA 92014, 800/243-7259.

©1998 Tehabi Books. All rights reserved. First printing. Printed in Korea.

10 9 8 7 6 5 4 3 2 1

Library of Congress Cataloging-in-Publication Data

Doolittle, Bill, 1948–
    The Kentucky Derby: run for the roses / by Bill Doolittle; foreword by Walter Cronkite
        p. cm.
    Includes index.
    ISBN 0-7370-0032-5 (hardcover).—ISBN 0-7370-0048-1 (pbk.).—ISBN 1-887656-15-4 (leatherbound)
    1. Kentucky Derby, Louisville, Ky. 2. Kentucky Derby, Louisville, Ky.—Pictorial works. I. Title.
    SF357.K4D66 1998
    798.4'009769'44—dc21   98-31311
                                CIP

Time-Life Books is a division of Time Life Inc.

TIME LIFE INC.
    George Artandi
    President and CEO

TIME-LIFE CUSTOM PUBLISHING
    Terry Newell
    Vice President and Publisher

    Neil Levin
    Vice President of Sales and Marketing

    Jennie Halfant
    Project Manager

    Jennifer Pearce
    Director of Acquisitions

    Liz Ziehl
    Director of Special Markets

Time Life is a trademark of Time Warner Inc. U.S.A.

EXHILARATION!
THE KENTUCKY DERBY, 1993

J ockey Jerry Bailey waves to the crowd as he crosses the finish line first aboard Sea Hero in the 1993 Kentucky Derby. From their Derby boxes, owner Paul Mellon and trainer MacK (short for MacKenzie) Miller experienced the thrill of a lifetime as they watched Bailey guide Sea Hero inside, outside, around, and past the field on the way to victory.

Three-time Derby-winning jockey Gary Stevens, clad in the blue and orange silks of owner Michael Tabor, accepts the special bouquet of roses he earned by scoring with Tabor's longshot, Thunder Gulch, in 1995. Stevens also won aboard Winning Colors in 1988 and Silver Charm in 1997.

CONTENTS

Jockey Pat Day felt the ultimate thrill of victory when he won the 1992 Kentucky Derby aboard Lil E. Tee. But he considered it more than a personal win in the world's greatest horse race. A devout Christian, Day dedicated the triumph to his faith. "Many times I had referred to my riding ability as a 'God-given talent,'" said Day. "Then I began to think about what that really meant."

The Kentucky Derby. What is it about the "Run for the Roses" that so captures our imagination, that tugs at our heartstrings, that makes us want to be in Kentucky for the Derby on the first Saturday in May?

Surely the Kentucky Derby is an anachronism. The race made sense when it was first staged in 1875. In those days, people's lives revolved around horses—there were horses to ride, horses to pull wagons, and sleek thoroughbreds who became the sporting heroes of the day. But today, the nearest most people come to horses is the horsepower in our automobiles. Yet our fascination with racehorses and the Kentucky Derby endures.

Fans who follow baseball, football, and basketball also find themselves interested in sporting events that are unique unto themselves—and especially those steeped in tradition. They'll always pause from reading the day-to-day box scores to watch The Masters, or the Indianapolis 500, or the Kentucky Derby. Those viewing the Derby on television somehow feel—if only for a moment—a part of the nostalgia of Old Kentucky.

TRIUMPH AND TRADITION

And those who attend the event in person sense they are there to witness history in the making.

For avid horse racing fans, the search for good seats begins months before the Derby. The younger set simply pay general admission on the day of the race to enjoy a festive lark in the infield, unperturbed by their slim chance to even glimpse a racehorse. Celebrities attend fabulous parties, and millions enjoy entertaining guests at home to watch the event unfold on television. For all Kentuckians, the Derby is a day in the sunshine and a moment in the limelight.

For the dedicated horseplayer, the fascination of the Derby is probably the degree of difficulty in picking the winner. But for the horse people, the Kentucky Derby is the dream of a lifetime, with a chance to catch the brass ring of racing immortality.

The Derby has always been a favorite of the sporting press. From the beginning, newspapers delivered first-hand accounts of the race and the flavor of Derby Week doings. Years ago, the Associated Press always cleared its "A Wire" as the time approached for the Kentucky Derby, set to flash the news of the Derby triumph around the world. Radio came along to give the event immediacy, and television brought us even closer to the action.

For most of us, I suspect, it is simply the beauty and drama of the Kentucky Derby that we find so alluring. It begins in the stables during the days leading up to the Derby, and ends with the shouting climax of the race itself— "Go Baby, Go!" Along the way are sprinkled events of grace and hospitality that are uniquely American in character. For many years, my wife, Betsy, and I have been the guests of the Barry Binghams of Louisville and also of Mary Lou Whitney, who with her late husband, C.V. Whitney, raced horses and owns a thoroughbred breeding farm in the heart of the Bluegrass country. Our friendship with Mary Lou goes back to the days when I worked for the United Press wire service and she was with the *Kansan* newspaper. I know that for so many Derby fans the renewal of old friendships is at the heart of their Derby experience.

There is no denying the color and vitality of the Kentucky Derby. A mixture of people from every walk of life converges on Churchill Downs for the running of the race. The stands are packed from the Skye Terrace high above the finish line to the furlongs of box seats in the ancient wooden grandstand—with thousands more spectators spread across the acres of brick and grass grounds. Late in the afternoon, a brilliant bugle sounds the call to the post for the Kentucky Derby. Famous jockeys in their brightly colored silks guide their magnificent horses as thousands sing "My Old Kentucky Home."

I have seen the spectacle and looked out across the panorama. I have felt the thrill of being a part of one of the world's greatest sporting events—and a part of a wonderful American tapestry. It is with a swelling of pride and a lifted spirit that I witness these momentous gatherings in celebration of will and triumph and tradition.

—WALTER CRONKITE

Walter Cronkite, with his wife, Betty (center), and Mary Lou Whitney.

TWIN SPIRES
CHURCHILL DOWNS

*G*olden morning sunshine reflects off the slate roof and highlights the century-old Twin Spires of Churchill Downs. These elegant wooden spires symbolize grace and tradition in Kentucky and have become so identified with the Kentucky Derby that Churchill Downs holds a copyright on the use of the words "Twin Spires."

The crocus pops up one day in February when the temperature suddenly jumps up above 60 degrees. People sneak out of work early and drive home with their car windows rolled down. Moms steer strollers through neighborhood stroller jams, and kids stay out playing ball till long after the sun goes down.

That night, the forsythia bushes go to work. Always just a step behind the crocus, they still manage to shake off winter hibernation in mere hours, and by morning that old brown forsythia bush is suddenly budding bright yellow. Everything that is not red or white or purple or yellow is simply green—including the bluegrass—and it all grows like crazy when sunshine breaks a path between thunderstorms.

These are the floral harbingers of spring in Kentucky, and the official start of Derby Fever.

My Old Kentucky Home

It makes no difference that two days later the temperature drops back to 40 degrees and the cold rain resumes. Things are underway for another Kentucky Derby.

The Derby has everything: It is colorful, sporty, and fun; it is as rare as gold and as common as corn; and it is all about drama and legends and history being made. It's a big-time sports event, and people love that.

They say you can travel to the ends of the earth, to Tibet or Timbuktu, and you'll find folks who have heard of the Kentucky Derby. The Derby belongs to every Kentuckian—and they like it so much that they can't wait to invite the rest of the world to become a part owner.

On the tracks and horse farms in Kentucky, people are waking out of sleep earlier, eager for the start of a new day. The everyday men and women of Kentucky, who have real jobs and work in office buildings and factories are ready for a big celebration to honor the return of spring.

The horses also know that it is spring. They're friskier, happier, more eager. They wake up an hour before the sun—before the morning birds, and even before the barn rooster—demanding to get out of their stalls and onto the racetrack.

As a rite of spring, curious newspaper and TV reporters,

taking time off from covering the mundane, stop by the Churchill Downs greenhouse to ask their perennial question about the tulips. Years ago, it was Churchill Downs gardener Donnie Lord who would field the queries. The reporters would ask, "Donnie, how do you get these tulips to bloom precisely on Derby Day every year?"

"Oh, it's all luck," Donnie always answered.

Then they'd edge in a little closer, drop their voices, and ask again, this time looking for the inside story.

"How do you do it, really?"

"I'm telling you, it's all luck," Donnie said.

And maybe it is.

SPRINGTIME
KEENELAND RACE COURSE

The beautiful colors of springtime in Kentucky: Redbud and dogwood burst forth along the rail at Keeneland Race Course. Keeneland runs a one-month race meeting in April, highlighted by the Toyota Blue Grass Stakes, a major prep for the Derby.

Above: The groom is the horse's closest friend, the person who takes care of the athlete through thick and thin, victories and losses, warm and cold, good days and bad.

Right: The double Ds stand for Darby Dan Farm, owner of Kentucky Derby winners Chateaugay (1963) and Proud Clarion (1967). The water bucket has a flat side so that it will stay level while hanging on the wall of the horse's stall.

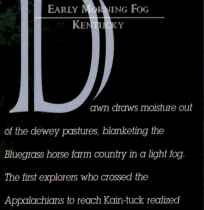

EARLY MORNING FOG
KENTUCKY

Dawn draws moisture out
of the dewey pastures, blanketing the
Bluegrass horse farm country in a light fog.
The first explorers who crossed the
Appalachians to reach Kain-tuck realized
what a wonderful natural pastureland they

Prior to the Revolutionary War, American colonists on the Eastern Seaboard heard of the land of Kentucky from explorers, and sought the way there. Those most interested were Virginians—people ready to go, ready to do, looking for new lands to call their own. Their business was raising livestock—horses, sheep, cattle—and they were enthralled with tales of a wonderful natural pastureland on the other side of the Appalachians, tales brought back by men like Daniel Boone and John Filson.

In 1784, Filson described a land the Indians called Kain-tuck. No Indian tribes resided in the area; all tribes agreed to leave the land free for all to hunt. Filson wrote, "Here is a great plenty of fine cane on which the cattle [native bison] feed and grow fat. . . . Where no cane grows there is abundance of wild rye, clover, and buffalo grass, covering vast tracts of country, and affording excellent food for cattle. The fields are covered with abundance of wild herbage not common to other countries."

Today the Bluegrass region, centering in the counties around Lexington, is filled with beautiful horse farms in a parklike setting. Grassy fields roll over small hills and meadows, divided by fences and narrow lanes, and intersected by little spring-fed creeks.

The farms have names like Claiborne, Calumet, Lane's End, Hermitage, and Spendthrift. In those pastures and barns are located the finest thoroughbreds and other breeds of horses. Some of those horses have been bought and sold for millions of dollars, and some cannot be purchased for any price.

Several years back, the late standardbred horse breeder Frederick Van Lennep sat in a leather armchair in his study at Castleton Farm, talking late into the night about the horse world of the Bluegrass.

"This land has always been a place where grazing animals lived," said Van Lennep. "There was grass here, and cane and water. And the open meadows had woods nearby where horses could find sanctuary from predators. A mare could hide in the woods while foaling.

"There is no proof of this," he said. "It is just something I believe: I think that even before white men arrived, horses had already been here. Perhaps they were wild horses who found their way here from the southwest. They would have been from those original horses brought to America by the Spanish—the mustangs you find living wild out west today. And maybe even horses from centuries ago. The ancestors of the modern horse. I can't prove it, but I think horses have always come here to this place."

The old Oakland racecourse thrived as a pre-Civil War racetrack in Louisville and was the site of the famous 1839 match race between Kentucky-owned Grey Eagle and Tennessee-owned Wagner. Wagner won the big race, and carried the glory back to his home state.

P A KINGDOM FOR THE HORSE
KENTUCKY

*icturesque four-rail white fences
section off grassy pastures at a Kentucky
horse farm. The lane between pastures
allows passage for horses and machines.
Safety is the primary concern in curving the
fence corners.*

MARE AND FOAL
KENTUCKY

Moments after birth, a newborn foal is up and standing by its mother's side. Within days, the pair is out and about in the pasture—first with a walk, then with a trot, then a gallop. After a few months of growing, the foal is "weaned" from his dam. Most thoroughbreds are born in the spring and weaned in the fall. On January 1, they all have their first birthday and become yearlings. One year later, at age two, they will go to the track to race.

Y Yearlings
  Kentucky

earlings frolic in the
field at Claiborne Farm, near Paris,
Kentucky. This is a time for growth and
testing swift legs in gallops across the fields.

There is no finer place to be on Earth, and there is nothing better that could be done than to fall happily into the throes of Kentucky tradition and Derby sporting excitement. It has often been said that if there were not already a Kentucky Derby, it would be necessary to invent one. The place is perfect. The time is perfect. The attitude is perfect. It is Derby time in Kentucky.

A handful of people planned the first Kentucky Derby, and today, thousands of citizens combine in a huge effort—from hot dog vendors to track brass—to put on the event in the grand style for which it is famous. But it's almost like the whole thing would happen anyway. Like spontaneous combustion: one pent up mass of color, ready to riot.

THE DAYS OF THE DERBY

T he Kentucky Derby is a
day in the sunshine for happy racing fans,
and a moment in the limelight for all
Kentuckians. The word "derby" is recognized
all over the world.

One month it's drizzly late winter, and the next month skyrockets are blasting off above the city. Balloons drift across the morning sky. Thousands of runners dash down a park hillside and ramble into the heart of the city in a mini-marathon. Steamboats churn their way up and down the Ohio River in an old-fashioned steamboat race—their pilots cheating and conniving (all perfectly legal)—in celebration of a time gone by. Everyone is doing something: Majorettes twirl, chefs cook, hostesses greet old friends, handicappers select, college students race rats, hoteliers turn down their best sheets, thousands of guests arrive, pickpocketing enjoys a once-a-year flourish, captains of industry entertain, a whole lot of cash changes hands . . . and THEN they run the races. When it is all over, everyone is worn out and satisfied.

• • •

The Kentucky Derby springs from a business decision made more than 125 years ago.

Kentucky horse breeders, a little down on their luck after the Civil War, decided they would stage a big-money thoroughbred horse race in the state's largest city to focus attention on their industry.

The idea was that the Kentucky Derby would be more than a horse race; it would be a spectacular event, and a ready excuse to have a good time. The key ingredient would be to run the very best horses in a classic race. That would set people talking, and the rest could be naturally built around the climactic event.

The Kentucky Derby has not always been held on the first Saturday in May. The first one came on Wednesday, May 17, 1875, and all agree the choice of a May date was a terrific pick. It's too hot in Louisville in the summer, too cold in the winter. And basketball begins in the fall.

AN EVENT IN ASCENDANCY
THE KENTUCKY DERBY, 1875-1998

The Kentucky Derby was first run in 1875 before a crowd of 10,000 fans, which was, to that time, the most people ever gathered in one place in the history of Kentucky. There were up years—and some forgettable down years around the turn of the century—but after Colonel Matt J. Winn took over in 1902, the Kentucky Derby experienced a steady rise in popularity. But it was in the late 1960s that the race really took off in terms of attendance.

For many years, the Derby Day crowd was always announced by Churchill Downs officials as 100,000. Maybe it had not always been quite that much, and maybe some years it was more. But pinning an actual figure on this Derby or that was not the point. The number 100,000 was huge, and so was the Derby crowd every year. And that huge number was firmly set in the consciousness of sportswriters and the racing public. 100,000. Period.

But then the actual turnstile count began to rise dramatically, and the track began to release figures that stamped the Derby as a sporting event in ascendancy. In 1969, 106,000 saw undefeated Majestic Prince win the Derby over a crack field. In 1971, 123,000 witnessed the unbelievable upset delivered by an unknown horse named Canonero II. And 130,000 were on hand to see Riva Ridge win the roses in 1972.

That set the stage for Secretariat—and the big red chestnut colt delivered. A new record 134,000 fans crowded into Churchill Downs in 1973 expecting—maybe just hoping—to see something special.

Colonel Matt J. Winn, 1930

GRANDSTAND
CHURCHILL DOWNS

One of the biggest stars of the Kentucky Derby is Churchill Downs itself. Even though it was built more than a century ago, the Churchill Downs grandstand is never called "old"; rather, it is "ancient" or "historic," implying that it has weathered the test of time and outlasted any newer models.

Originally, a grandstand and small clubhouse were built on the opposite side of the track, where the barns are today. But that left fans looking into the sun, and exposed them to cold winds blowing in from the north and west. In order to solve this problem, a new grandstand was constructed on the west side of the track during 1894 and '95. It left fans shaded from the sun and sheltered from the elements.

The new Churchill Downs of 1895 was designed by twenty-four-year-old Louisvillian Joseph Baldez, who topped his design with a sublime pair of perfect spires. Over the past century, Churchill Downs has added on to that original 285-foot-long grandstand many times, but the Twin Spires remain the visible center of a sporting shrine recognized worldwide.

The seating at the Downs is unique in that from one end of the grandstand to the other—more than a quarter mile now—the main third-floor level seats are all enclosed in boxes of six seats each. Fans don't just get seats for the Kentucky Derby, they buy a box.

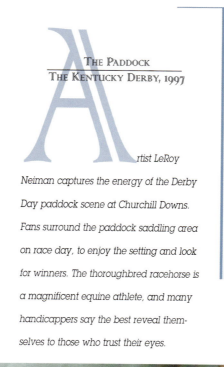

THE PADDOCK
THE KENTUCKY DERBY, 1997

Artist LeRoy Neiman captures the energy of the Derby Day paddock scene at Churchill Downs. Fans surround the paddock saddling area on race day, to enjoy the setting and look for winners. The thoroughbred racehorse is a magnificent equine athlete, and many handicappers say the best reveal themselves to those who trust their eyes.

"Ben Ali" winner of Kentucky Derby

Years after seeing the first Kentucky Derby, Colonel Matt J. Winn became the president of Churchill Downs and refined the May date, determining to set one certain day for the race to be run each year. He wanted to establish a tradition, and he wanted a good day for it.

Winn studied the weather conditions of previous Derbies, researched the Louisville weather records as far back as he could. He found that the first Saturday in May was most often the prettiest day of spring. Oh, some years it might rain, or it might be cold—heck, even a few snow flakes have been spotted— but most Derby Days are like this: clear, sunny, 75 degrees. It usually rains just days before the Derby, which encourages the springtime greenery and peps up the track. With the sunshine, tulip bulbs pop up in a matter of hours to appear just in time for Derby Day.

More than 10,000 fans attended the first Derby, which was, up to that time, the most people ever collected in one spot in Kentucky. Newspapers reported that a cloud of dust hung over the city in the days leading up to the race, as people from far and wide arrived to be a part of the event. And on race day, May 17, 1875, the streets were packed with people and horses headed for the new track outside of Louisville.

"The mule-drawn street cars were loaded to the limit," recalled Winn, who wasn't yet a full Kentucky Colonel in charge of Churchill Downs, but only a wide-eyed Louisville boy of thirteen when he attended his first Derby. "Those who had horses, hitched them to carts, or buggies, and were on their way. Others horse-backed to the track, while thousands walked."

Over the decades, most things have remained constant. The horses, the excitement, the gaiety, the colors of spring, the thrill of one's very first Derby.

"The first Derby Day I remember as if it were yesterday, . . ." Winn recalled in 1944, the year of his seventieth consecutive Derby.

ON THE BRICKS
DERBY DAY, THEN AND NOW

*M*any fans love being "on the bricks"—Churchill Down's brick-covered ground floor—on Derby Day. A University of Louisville Speed Scientific School student once calculated that there are enough bricks on the floor of the Downs to cover the entire Empire State Building.

Although the spectators who graced the clubhouse grounds of yesteryear, above, waited for odds to be displayed on a large chalkboard instead of an electric one, they did so with a bit more elbow room than today's fans, left.

"My father decided to be there [for the opening]. He wasn't a horse player. But this was more than a race day. It was a festival, and my father felt he ought to be at the track to see if the 'goings on' would be worth all the fuss the people had been making about the new track, and the new kind of racing. . . .

"I was up at dawn," Winn continued. "It was clear, sunshiny and warm. Father hitched the horse to the wagon, which he generally used in hauling groceries from the wholesale houses, and we were off for my first Derby through the greatest traffic jam Louisville had known up to that time."

Winn's view of the first Derby was from the infield.

"It was a thrill for me, this first Derby, with crowds swirling around in the infield, the grandstand a riot of color, and tenseness in some places, unrestrained enthusiasm elsewhere, as the time neared for the horses to parade to the starting line in readiness for the race that all Louisville, and most of Kentucky had discussed for so many months. I don't suppose I was the only 13 year old boy in the infield, but I guess, by sitting on the seat of my father's wagon, and then standing on it during the running of the Derby, I had the best view of any 13 year old boy."

SILKS
THE SPORT OF KINGS, 1762

A long time ago somebody called horse racing the Sport of Kings. That was in England, where King Charles II and his royal pals put together the first racing meets, and worried about such lofty issues as "improving the breed." Since it was really hard to recognize one's horse from across a meadow, in 1762 the dukes and lords adopted racing silks—in colors—for their jocks to wear, so they could tell how the horses were doing in the races. Those original silks still exist today. Several years back, in 1985,

the present-day Lord Derby shipped a horse named Teleprompter from England to Chicago to win the Arlington Million. When jockey Tony Ives crossed under the finish line first aboard Teleprompter, he sported the ancient Lord Derby's silks: black, with white cap.

So, the title is correct. The racing sport of old England was, and to some extent still is, the Sport of Kings. But in America, it is simply a sport enjoyed by everyone.

And in Kentucky, the horse is king.

T
MEDIA
DERBY WEEK

The backside of Churchill Downs teems with print and television reporters as well as photographers during Derby Week. The track grants more than two thousand media credential requests each Derby, and throws the place open for reporters to dig up stories that reach racing fans all around the world. The sports writers watch the works, talk to the trainers and owners, trade tales with each other, and scarf down plenty of free food and drinks. They stare in awe at sleek racehorses, and inhale the horse barn smells of liniment, manure, and coffee. They locate special secret spies to provide them with inside dope. They listen intently to what is being said, and then try to make sense of it all.

Colonel Matt J. Winn, who ran Churchill Downs from 1902 until his death in 1949, understood the importance of having these interpreters on hand. He cultivated nationally syndicated newspaperwriters, even to the extent of setting up a New York headquarters in the off-season, where he worked the scribes.

Commemorative lapel pin

He would see the writers at ballgames and prize fights, and remember to invite them to be on hand for the Kentucky Derby. He passed on tips and tales, and always picked up the dinner checks and bar tabs of big-time writers like Damon Runyon and Grantland Rice. "Give me the five best writers in New York," said Winn, "and you can have the rest."

Over the years, the best writers did, indeed, find their way to Churchill Downs. William Faulkner spent a week on the backside at the Downs in 1955, chronicling the training of Derby favorite Nashua and drinking in (literally and figuratively) what the Derby experience is all about. Today, the famous horse scribes still can't resist an invitation to cover the Derby, even when they can claim no expertise on the subject.

"I don't know a thing in the world about this," admitted Dave Kindred of The Sporting News. "But I love it"

T

oday's thoroughbred racehorse is the culmination of three hundred years of selective breeding—mixing and mating bloodlines to create the ideal racing animal. Every thoroughbred has its own pedigree, a carefully cataloged chart of all of its ancestors. It's the equine equivalent of a birth certificate—only a lot more detailed. When a horse wins the Kentucky Derby, its pedigree is meticulously analyzed to see where it all went right.

GO FOR GIN
THE KENTUCKY DERBY, 1994

Saturday, May 7, 1994, was a dark and rainy day. The track was sloppy, but Go for Gin (left) didn't get a speck of mud on him as he surged to the front early to win the 120th Kentucky Derby.

"To some of us, the echoes of the old starting drums still linger over the ancient Downs. The rustle of taffeta, the sense of a world apart, the gentle laughter, the rebel scarlet silk of the Lost Cause, and the reverence for the thoroughbred are there like an unseen mist, an unforgettable aura when you're a part of it for the first time."

—Bill Corum, President of Churchill Downs, 1950–'54

There are many traditions of the Kentucky Derby—mint juleps, exciting parties, the singing of "My Old Kentucky Home" as the horses parade to post. But the greatest of all Derby traditions is probably just tradition itself.

The Run for the Roses

It's the tradition of fathers taking sons to their first Kentucky Derby and young ladies shopping for their first Derby dress.

It's lavish parties and glamorous celebrities—and ordinary people who like to celebrate the Derby, too. It's a big parade, and an old-fashioned steamboat race, and lawns that sparkle green across the city.

Derby tradition is all the people who make a pilgrimage to Louisville on the first Saturday in May: Old guys who saw Citation win—and Native Dancer lose. And it is beautiful women, college kids, and powerful tycoons. It's all about million-dollar thoroughbreds and high-stakes wagers and tossing a buck in a hat and pulling out the name of a horse that might win the Kentucky Derby.

Long ago, before the mint julep became a famous symbol of fast racehorses and the good life in Kentucky, there was fine bourbon whisky in the sideboard and fresh green mint growing wild along the creek outside the house. One day, nobody knows just when, the whisky and the mint were mated. Sugar and ice were added, the whole thing was served in a silver cup, and the mint julep was born.

Over time, the mint julep and the Kentucky Derby have

grown to become inseparable Kentucky traditions. Inexperienced bartenders, not yet possessing a sense of art, hate to make mint juleps, and their concoctions reflect their disdain. Traditionalists dote over their julep recipes and produce handcrafted juleps that cause them to swell with pride when they present them to customers. At the track, the juleps are sold by the thousands, and served in Derby mint julep glasses. Surprisingly, the track juleps are wonderful.

All agree that a mint julep is not an easy drink to make. But it's worth the effort, says Louisvillian Jim Hennessy.

"It is my personal opinion that the mint julep is the greatest drink for Derby Week that has ever been invented," Hennessy said. "I wouldn't give you ten cents for one the other fifty-one weeks of the year, but for some reason . . . well, I'll tell you that I like having a cocktail here and there, and I love beer. But a mint julep is like a flower in spring to me.

"Maybe it's the frost that comes up on the outside of the silver

VICTORY ROSES
THE KENTUCKY DERBY, 1913

After Donerail won the 1913 Kentucky Derby, he wouldn't stand still to have a rose blanket draped across his shoulders. But jockey Roscoe Goose, who acted as an assistant trainer for the horse, as well as his rider, knew what to do. He dismounted, removed the saddle, and clambered back aboard. For whatever reason, it worked, and Donerail stood calmly as he received the winner's rose blanket and had his picture taken. Above is T. P. Hayes, the breeder, owner, and trainer of Donerail.

1919 Fall Meet poster features Sir Barton, that year's Derby winner

cup," Hennessy continued. "It's a very attractive drink. When you stick that mint in there and the cup starts frosting, and you sprinkle the white powdered sugar on the green mint . . . well, you simply cannot find a better presentation than the mint julep. It just looks good."

Another good-looking tradition is the springtime blooms that blanket the city.

The flowering trees and shrubs of springtime Louisville —the forsythia, dogwood, and redbud—lead the floral parade into spring. But by Derby Day, tulips and azaleas and irises have marched to the forefront. They are everywhere—at the track and in Louisville yards from Portland to Prospect.

But no flower is more important to the Kentucky Derby than the rose. The flower and the race have always been connected—back to the first Derbies, when newspaper accounts noted that Colonel Meriwether Lewis Clark highlighted his Derby Day attire with a beautiful rose in his lapel.

Nowadays the Kroger Company, a large grocery chain, produces the official rose garland for the winner of the Kentucky Derby. The store invites the public to witness the making of the rose garland, which includes 554 roses, set in 554 tiny vials of water sewn into a 2-1/2-yard-long green satin blanket the night before the Derby. The special creation is transported to the track on Derby morning with a police escort, and is kept in a refrigerated truck until the Derby race is run.

Before Kroger became the official sponsor of the rose blanket, the blanket was made by Mrs. Betty Walker Korfhage, who followed in the tradition of her mother, Mrs. Kingsley Walker. It was her family's florist shop that created the traditional design for the Derby rose blanket.

The first winner to have a blanket of roses draped across his shoulders was His Eminence, ridden by Jimmy Winkfield in 1901. The roses were red and white, and the jockey was also awarded a rose bouquet. The tradition of a special bouquet for the winning rider continues, and the jockey will sometimes present individual roses to special friends and those in the

MINT JULEPS
A KENTUCKY DERBY TRADITION

Mint julep stories spring up as plentifully as the mint weed itself. One wag observed that, "In Kentucky, the corn is full of kernels, and the Colonels full of corn."

This old Derby mint julep tale is based on the one told by the late Derby historian Jim Bolus. It seems special guests of Colonel Clark's for an early Derby were Countess Helena Modjeska, of Poland, and her husband, Count Bozenta Chlapowski. Clark invited a few local luminaries for a Derby Day breakfast and made the countess the Guest of Honor. Clark prepared a mint julep mixture of his own recipe in a huge silver bowl for all the guests to enjoy. With much pomp, he had the silver punch bowl placed in front of Countess Helena. She smiled, then suddenly took the big bowl in both hands and sipped the drink.

"My dear Colonel Clark! Eet ees supreme!" she exclaimed. "Won't you please feex another such dreenk for ze Count?"

So now you know you don't have to limit yourself to just one mint julep. In fact, an old saying once evaluated the proper levels of julep consumption like this:

"One is plenty,
Two is too many,
and three ain't near enough."

stable of the winning horse.

Actually, the rose blanket tradition could have started three years earlier—if Lieber Karl had won the Derby. Mrs. John Schorr had arranged for a rose blanket to be made for her husband's horse. But old Lieber Karl lost the race to Plaudit.

The phrase "Run for the Roses" was coined by *New York Journal* columnist Bill Corum in 1925. This was in the day when Ty Cobb was the "Georgia Peach," and the "Four Horsemen of the Apocalypse" rode out of the Notre Dame backfield. Nicknames like those caught the public's imagination, and "Run for the Roses" became forever identified with the Kentucky Derby.

The most exotic rose tale is that of New York socialite and gambler E. Barry Wall, who became so delighted with being present for the 1883 Derby that he telegraphed to New York to have a railroad carload of roses sent to him in Louisville in time for the Derby. In the post-race party, after Leonatus won, Wall graciously handed bouquets of roses to all the ladies present.

And not just any roses. Wall insisted on a new rose he had seen in a New York show called the American Beauty. Today, the rose specified for the Derby blanket is the Visa rose, but the American Beauty is still THE rose of roses.

Parties have always been a part of Derby tradition, and, needless to say, they range from ragged to rich—but always fun.

For many years, the gala to end all galas has been the Derby Eve bash at Hamburg Place, in Lexington, hosted by Anita and Preston Madden. The word "lavish" does not really do a Madden party justice. Months of planning go into the event, and dancers and bands and decorations are all choreographed to produce a fantasy illusion. The Madden party is by invitation, but the guests pay $250 each to attend. The proceeds go to a local charity.

Tickets are a pricey $600 to the charity gala hosted by Patricia Barnstable Brown and her husband, David Brown, at their home in the Louisville Highlands. The Brown party has been visited by many entertainers and celebrities, including General Norman Schwarzkopf, just home from triumph in the Gulf War.

Of course the Derby is not just for the rich and famous. It's an occasion for everyone to have a ball.

RECIPE
DERBY WEEK

If you are looking for a mint julep recipe, here is the one the track concessioneers use for Derby Week: Combine 8,000 quarts of whisky; 60 tons of crushed snow ice; 150 bushels of fresh mint; and a secret amount of sugar made into simple syrup.

Of all the winners of all
the races at Churchill Downs each year,
only the Kentucky Derby winner is led into
the special horseshoe-shaped winner's circle
in the infield at Churchill Downs. Overbrook
Farm owner William T. Young and daughter
Lucy Young Boutin hold the reins of their
1996 Derby winner Grindstone. For jockey
Jerry Bailey it was the second visit to the
Kentucky Derby Winner's Circle.

On weekdays before the Derby, office workers pour out of their towers at noontime and head for the Derby Festival Chow Wagon. The breakfast joints are jammed, and most bars roar on till 4 A.M. Seeking quieter corners, hard-case handicappers pore over the *Daily Racing Form* and argue the merits of horses and jockeys, then see how all that study pays off the next day at the track. Some people take the week off just to enjoy the festivities. But many work extra hours to capture as much green as possible while the cash is flowing. A cabbie can make a ton of cash on Derby Day, and a top waiter can clear a grand the night before.

Some folks never go near the racetrack, but will tell you that there's no time like Derby time for having a ball. Rock groups and country warblers pack 'em in at concerts and night clubs. And the guys who pick horses for a living make enough dough advising "clients" to finance their own plays for the week. Even after it's all over, the Honorable Order of Kentucky Colonels and the governor of Kentucky hold a big Sunday brunch on the grounds of the Wickland estate in Bardstown.

Naturally, all this fun spills over to the rest of the world. One of the biggest out-of-town Derby parties ever thrown took place at the King Ranch in Texas in 1996. The occasion

marked the fiftieth anniversary of Assault's 1946 Kentucky Derby victory. Assault, who went on to win the Triple Crown and became one of the big sports heroes of his day, was one of three King Ranch horses to win the Derby. The others were Middleground and Bold Venture. The hosts ordered Derby mint julep glasses shipped in by the caseload from Louisville for the event. They did not have to send off for Kentucky bourbon. They have that in healthy supply in Texas.

Mary Frentz Bellino's famous New York City Derby parties never rivaled the Texas King Ranch bash in magnitude, but the hostess was renowned for successfully bringing a bit of Old Kentucky to the island of Manhattan.

"In any party," the hostess explained, "the most important thing is the people, and you want to lace your Derby party with Kentuckians. They'll demand respect for the event and get all teary-eyed— and they know the words to the song."

EVE OF THE ROSES
DERBY GALAS

*F*estive fun and a swirl of bright colors characterize the gala atmosphere of Derby Week parties.

Do not be deceived, the pilots of the boats cheat in the Great Steamboat Race. The match comes on Wednesday of Derby Week, and more than 100,000 people line the banks of the Ohio to view the event. Hundreds more are crowded onto the racing boats—which lights up the "Inquiry" sign right there: If victory is paramount, why do they load on all those passengers?

But no one seems to care.

The principal contestants are Louisville's own excursion sternwheeler, the Belle of Louisville, and the Delta Queen of Cincinnati. The Belle is smaller than the Delta Queen, which is a true traveling hotel that plies the Ohio and Mississippi Rivers from Cincinnati to New Orleans. The Mississippi Queen has also participated in the race, as has the Julia Belle Swain, out of her Illinois River port in Peoria.

If there were no room for cheating in this race, the much more powerful Delta Queen would be far ahead in the race series. Instead, the two river boats are near dead even in victories; the traditional rack of antlers hung on the pilot house of the last winner has been passed back and forth many times.

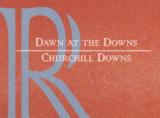

Rays of the early morning sunshine reflect on an empty grandstand at Churchill Downs. On Derby Day, more than 140,000 people will fill the grounds for another renewal of the world's most famous horse race.

Dawn at the Downs
Churchill Downs

112

FINISH

Celebration!
The Skies over Louisville

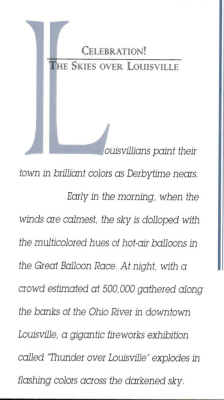

Louisvillians paint their town in brilliant colors as Derbytime nears.

Early in the morning, when the winds are calmest, the sky is dolloped with the multicolored hues of hot-air balloons in the Great Balloon Race. At night, with a crowd estimated at 500,000 gathered along the banks of the Ohio River in downtown Louisville, a gigantic fireworks exhibition called "Thunder over Louisville" explodes in flashing colors across the darkened sky.

The tradition of the Kentucky Derby Festival began with a Derby Parade back in 1956. The parade is still a cornerstone of the festival and is held on Thursday of Derby Week.

There are many equestrian units in the parade, and for the hundreds and hundreds of band members, many of whom are city kids, it is an introduction to horses.

Derby Festival lapel pin

It is still four days before the race, but what happens on this morning, on an almost deserted racetrack, in what seems like the middle of the night, will become the single most important factor in realizing what the outcome of the big race will be on Saturday.

At five minutes past five o'clock in the morning, the winner of the 1986 Kentucky Derby is about to be revealed.

It's funny about the Derby. It's called the "Greatest Two Minutes in Sports," but what happens in those climatic two minutes depends so much on what has come before. Months before. And weeks before. And, in this case, just days before the Derby.

DOWN TO THE WIRE

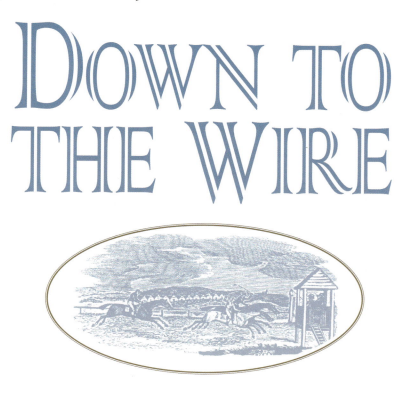

It was 5:05 A.M. on a Tuesday morning before the 1986 Kentucky Derby, and Charlie Whittingham, the famous horse trainer, then seventy-three, with a lifetime of victories salted away in his memory bank, was about to create that one moment that would get his horse into the Kentucky Derby winner's circle. That horse's name was Ferdinand.

Ferdinand was lightly considered by most professional handicappers for that Derby, and would eventually be sent off as a 17-1 long shot on Derby Day. But a few longtime followers of the sport respected Whittingham so much they had at least one eye on him—to see for themselves if he had some aces in his hand he hadn't yet shown. After all, Whittingham, the Hall-of-Fame trainer, had come to Louisville with only two previous Derby starters. In 1958, Gone Fishin' was eighth to Tim Tam, and in 1960, Divine Comedy was ninth to Venetian Way. But in the twenty-six years since Whittingham had last come to Kentucky with a Derby horse, he had always said the same thing: "I'm not coming back until I've got a horse that can win."

This is why a few hardy souls had gotten up in the dark of night to be at Churchill Downs at five in the morning: to see if this was The One.

Whittingham bounced around the barn and greeted the onlookers with a "howdy." Ferdinand was already up, and groom William Albritton was brushing the horse's red coat with long, smooth strokes while assistant trainer Larry Gilligan, an ex-jock and training assistant to Whittingham, worked with the saddles. A bare light bulb gleamed down from the ceiling of the old wooden barn, cracking the darkness with a little bit of light. Some of the light filtered into Ferdinand's stall, playing on his shiny coat. At about 5:20 A.M., a van pulled up and out stepped Bill Shoemaker, who would ride Ferdinand in the Derby.

The association of Shoemaker, fifty-four that year, and Whittingham is long standing. Together, they'd done everything—except collaborate on a Kentucky Derby victory. The Shoe looked in on Ferdinand, and then checked on Hidden Light, a filly he would ride for Whittingham in the Kentucky Oaks.

"Here's the way we'll do it," Whittingham began, affably filling the small audience in on the schedule of events for that morning's big workout for Ferdinand.

T
DAWN AT THE DOWNS
DERBY WEEK

here are reasons why horse people begin their days before the sun rises. One is that the horses are raring to get out on the track and stretch their legs. Another is that you can beat the heat by starting early in warm weather months. But the most important reason is that it's the way they've always done it.

DERBY MAGIC
THE KENTUCKY DERBY, 1986

Some people think it was all luck that jockey Bill Shoemaker found a tiny passageway through a wall of horses at the top of the stretch in the 1986 Kentucky Derby. A moment earlier, or a moment later, they say, and that hole would not have been there, and Shoemaker could not have sent Ferdinand into the clear and on to glory.

That day's winner, Ferdinand, owned by Mrs. Elizabeth Keck, was unexpected. He paid $37.40 to win. But you couldn't call it a surprise, and there was more than luck operating that day. Maybe it was fate that left a slim slant of daylight for the rider, or maybe it was skill. At the age of fifty-four, Bill Shoemaker knew that hole would open—and just when it would happen. The Derby victory was Shoemaker's fourth, and accounted for one of his record 8,833 career victories.

And while *The Shoe* was becoming the oldest Derby-winning jockey, Hall-of-Fame trainer *Charlie Whittingham*, at the age of seventy-three, was becoming the oldest trainer ever to triumph in the Derby. Three years later, Whittingham would break his own record with another Derby winner.

Two old guys and a fresh-faced three-year-old colt. It wasn't luck, and it was more than skill. It was Derby magic.

Whittingham said Ferdinand would work "in company" with the filly, Hidden Light, and "break off" from the five-eighths pole, which is about the middle of the backstretch. Ferdinand would begin about three lengths behind Hidden Light, to "give him something to run at."

Over on the front side of Churchill Downs, through the tunnel underneath the grandstand, Ferdinand and Hidden Light arrived together at the paddock. And then something totally perplexing became apparent. Shoemaker was riding Hidden Light, and Larry Gilligan was riding Ferdinand for the biggest workout of the horse's life. One could only figure that Whittingham knew what he was doing.

Onlookers clambered up the old wooden stairs to the third floor of the deserted grandstand, right under the Twin Spires, to see the horses take their first steps out onto the track and then break out of a walk.

The horses headed around the Clubhouse turn, gradually picking up speed. Shoemaker and Hidden Light took the lead, with Gilligan falling in a couple horse lengths back from the filly. As they neared the five-eighths pole over on the backstretch, everything happened in an instant. One moment they were going one speed, and the next moment they were flying!

Around the turn, Ferdinand picked it up and suddenly was on even terms with Hidden Light, as the pair turned for home with one-quarter mile to run to the wire.

Neither jock seemed to move a muscle, letting the horses do it all on their own, as they flew to the wire.

Click. One minute flat is an excellent time for a five-furlong work. A very fast workout is :59. Top-class horses will occasionally work in :58 "and change." Dr. Fager once commanded a headline on the back page of the Daily Racing Form when he worked five furlongs in :56. He was the fastest horse of his era.

I was hoping for :59 from Ferdinand when I looked at my watch. It read :57 2/5.

"Guess I got it a little quick," I said to fellow racing fan Joe D. Raine Jr.

"What did you get?"

"Fifty-seven and two-fifths."

Joe didn't say a word. He just showed me his watch. It read :57 2/5.

The workout time was officially reported by the professional clockers as :58 3/5. And, you know, their time was probably right.

But more than a second slower? Who knows—tales of phantom work times are part of the Romance of the Turf.

Exercise saddle and pad from the Bob Baffert barn

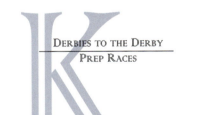

DERBIES TO THE DERBY
PREP RACES

Kentucky Derby contenders earn their tickets to Louisville by showing that they belong with the best in important prep races throughout the spring.

The big Derby prep races are rich and famous events on their own, fitting into a tableau that stretches across the country, including the Santa Anita Derby, Florida Derby, Louisiana Derby, Jim Beam Stakes, Lone Star Derby, Toyota Blue Grass Stakes, Arkansas Derby, and Wood Memorial.

Recently, a handful of Derby entrants have arrived in Kentucky from overseas, and Churchill Downs expects international participation in the Kentucky Derby to grow in the next quarter century.

M

ore than one fan has observed that horses are more pampered than people. Of course, the thoroughbreds wouldn't need such tender loving care if they were just left alone to be horses in a field. But to maintain a keen racing edge and stay sound through the stresses of training, the racehorse becomes a high-maintenance athlete.

WORKOUTS
CHURCHILL DOWNS

Most mornings of a horse's career are totally unremarkable. The horse is saddled, taken to the track, exercised in a long gallop, returned, walked to "cool out," and then washed and fed. Protective, padded bandages are wrapped around the lower legs, and the horse is "put up." Most mornings the trainer is asked, "How'd he look?" and will answer, "The same as yesterday." Then everybody goes to breakfast.

But workouts are different.

A workout is exercise at speed. In the old days, they called these workouts "trials." Over in England and Ireland and France, they have a way of training that involves working horses in company across broad, rolling pasturelands. Here in the States, the horses are all stabled in stalls in barns at the track. There are about 1,400 horses stabled at Churchill Downs during a race meet, and most of them are out every morning for exercise. But on certain mornings, maybe every seven days, or more often coming up to a big race, a horse will "work."

In a workout, a horse is first allowed to loosen up and stretch his legs in a light gallop that eventually takes him to the point on the track where the work will begin. As the horse realizes that this is going to be a workout, he gets "on the bit," champing to be turned loose. As horse and rider near that point, the horse is under a severe hold by the rider. Finally the rider makes the slightest pull on the left rein, steering the horse to the rail . . . and AWAY they go!

You love to see that eagerness, the instant acceleration, that lets you know the horse has its mind on running. Then you want to see his stride eat up ground, with more and more acceleration as the work progresses, finally hitting the wire in full stride and flying. He's then pulled up but, hard to slow down, is eager for more.

Now, every trainer has his or her own methods, and most vary their routines depending on the mental and physical makeup of the individual horse and what the racer has been doing lately. The whole idea is for a horse to put enough into the work to be "dead fit" on race day.

Getting into tip-top condition on Derby Day, and being ready to run the race of his life, is what this is all about. The actual time of the workout is far less important than the manner in which it is accomplished by the horse.

TIME CAPSULE
100TH KENTUCKY DERBY, 1974

Hall-of-Fame trainer Woodford C. Stephens—better known as Woody—always had trouble picking his greatest thrill from a career full of magic moments. When in New York, he might have mentioned winning five consecutive Belmont Stakes—an almost unbelievable achievement. But back home in Kentucky, his heart was with the Kentucky Derby, which he won with Cannonade in 1974 and Swale in 1984. "I guess winning the 100th Derby is my greatest thrill of all," said Stephens. "[Just] a country boy from Midway, Kentucky, and there I was, up on that victory stand with Princess Margaret for the 100th Derby."

The day of the Kentucky Derby is the culmination of a week of wondering and worrying, late nights and three-hours-till-dawn mornings, board room strategizing and just seeing what will happen. But Derby Week is merely the climax of many weeks leading up to the Derby Trail.

And the Derby Trail is actually many trails, leading from just about every racing center in the world to Churchill Downs.

For many horses, the journey to the Derby begins with a period of hibernation at the end of their two-year-old campaigns. A wise trainer will "put up" his star colt sometime in November and give it a few weeks of rest and relaxation. No races, no hard training, just a time to wind down and heal up nicks and soreness from the season's racing wars.

This is a time to grow and fill out. This period might be likened to adolescence in children, with the equine teenagers gaining in physical and mental maturity.

On January 1, all thoroughbreds have their official birthdays with two-year-olds graduating to their Derby year. Though most horses are born between February and May, a common date was long ago agreed upon for the sake of bookkeeping efficiency.

Come January, the top colts in the East will have wintered a bit in Florida or South Carolina, and then are sent back into serious training, with an eye on the prep races leading to the Kentucky Derby on the first Saturday in May.

This is a tough time on these youngsters. A lot fall by the wayside, simply unable to run with their faster peers or cope with the physical rigors of training for speed and distance. Young horses pick up all of the fevers and bugs going around, and that knocks them out of training. Every year, people ask, "Doesn't it seem like we've lost an awful lot of top prospects this year?"

The answer is yes, but that's the way it always is. It is a hard thing to get ready for the Derby, and that makes the prize even more difficult to secure.

For the horsemen, the search for a Derby horse is never ending. Most, of course, will never have a Derby horse, which are just too rare. But some people have more access to the top bloodstock and have a realistic chance of finding the pot of gold at the end of the rainbow.

INJURIES
KENTUCKY DERBY PREPARATION

Injuries are the biggest nemesis of racehorses, and particularly of three-year-old colts, who are being asked to run further in the Derby than they have ever run before in a race. A lot of strenuous training goes into preparing a horse for that kind of test.

Consider the horse as a racing machine. He is all strength and power through the girth, with huge lungs to take in enormous breaths of air to fuel strong muscles. But the huge chest and body, the engine, is all carried along on long, lean legs. And the longer and leaner the legs, the more ground a horse's stride will cover.

But that makes them fragile.

Try this: Reach down and try to put your fingers around your leg above your ankle. Then compare that to a horse's leg above the ankle. Not much difference—except the horse is carrying more than one thousand pounds of horse and rider.

Derby history is replete with the names of famous horses who almost made it to the Derby, but didn't. Graustark fractured his leg in the 1966 Blue Grass, and never ran again. Race favorites General Duke (1957) and Sir Gaylord (1962) broke down the day before the Derby, and A. P. Indy (1992) came up lame on the morning of Derby Day.

Hoof conditioner to prevent cracking

Taking a tight hold of the reins, the exercise rider allows the horse to gallop, but not run away in an all-out racing stride—as the horse would love to do. But while this gray racer is a mass of pent-up power, you can see it has manners and high class. It is not a struggle between horse and rider, but a study in the professional cooperation of man and beast.

KENTUCKY HORSES AND THE FIRST DERBY
THE NINETEENTH CENTURY

To understand how the Kentucky Derby came to be, you must travel back to the nineteenth century in America. The horse was the king of the highways, as well as the racetracks. The automobile had not yet been invented, and there were no tractors, either.

In the cities, deliveries were made by horses pulling wagons. Streetcars were pulled by horses or mules. The Overland Stage was powered by horses, and so was the surrey with the fringe on top. When the country doctor made a house call far from town, the doc could count on catching a nap on the way home. The horse knew the way. When it was time for fun, horse racing was the leading spectator sport in America.

In that setting, in the first half of the nineteenth century, Kentucky became the leading horse-breeding state—supplying the nation with horses.

But the Civil War (1861-65) nearly wiped out the horse business in Kentucky.

The war chewed up horses. By the thousands, horses died like men in battle—blown to bits by artillery and felled by hails of bullets. As a border state, Kentucky was drawn on for its horse supply by both Northern and Southern armies. At first the armies bought the horses, but there are many sad tales of breeding stock, too young or too old to ride, being stolen and ridden until they dropped. But there are also stories of a few prized stallions and mares ingeniously hidden from marauders. Those special survivors became the foundation sires and dams for rekindling ancient thoroughbred bloodlines.

The Kentucky horse farmers rebuilt their farms after the Civil War ended in 1865. But they had lost business to horse farms in the North. The breeders called upon Colonel Meriwether Lewis Clark, of Louisville, to dream up something that would refocus the eyes of the nation upon the Kentucky horse business.

Clark was the right man for the job. He was a grandson of William Clark, of the Lewis and Clark expedition, and a grandnephew of Revolutionary War hero General George Rogers Clark. He was a Louisville socialite, and knew a great deal about the world. Clark traveled to England to see the classic English races and found the doors to the "sport of kings" opened to him.

Clark also visited France, where he studied the French system of pari-mutuel betting, which means "betting amongst ourselves." The system was pioneered by Clark at Churchill Downs and today pari-mutuel wagering is the standard of horse race betting throughout North America.

Clark unveiled three feature races patterned on the English classics at his new track: the Kentucky Derby (for three-year-old horses, and "open to the world"); the Kentucky Oaks (for three-year-old fillies); and the Clark Handicap (for older horses).

Clark agreed with the Lexington breeders that the Kentucky Derby needed to be held in Louisville. For one thing, the breeders hoped to open a permanent racetrack in the state's largest city. But, more important, the founders wanted to locate the race where it was most accessible to fans from other parts of the country. In 1875, Louisville had already become an important railroad city, but more than that, it was a great riverboat town on the Ohio River.

This was the era of steamboat transportation, and the most prominent cities of mid-America were the big river cities of St. Louis, Cincinnati, and New Orleans. Cincinnati had established a music festival, New Orleans had the Mardi Gras, and Clark felt that a festival atmosphere would work well for Kentucky's big horse race.

In later years, special railroad cars would unload fans in Louisville, and today hundreds of private planes bring fans from all over the world.

And for the horse breeders, Clark's plan worked perfectly. The age of the working horse is past, but Kentucky remains at the top of the world in breeding the finest thoroughbred racing stock.

Joe Cotton, Kentucky-bred winner of the 1885 Derby

Louisville Jockey Club membership badge

And when that chance is there, it's all the trainers can think about.

"I remember a horse called Private Rite, that I had here in Florida," said top trainer Claude R. McGaughey III, who is universally known by the nickname Shug. "He looked like he was going to be all right, then ended up hurting himself. But he won an allowance race here in Miami, way off by himself, the first time going around two turns.

"That night we went to see . . ." and at this point McGaughey paused trying to remember the name of something besides a horse.

"Allison," McGaughey called down the shed row to his wife. "What was the name of that band we went to see with Dan Chandler in Miami that time?"

"The Eagles," Allison yelled back.

"The Eagles. Yeah. Well, all I could think about during that concert was that this was a horse that could have a chance to win the Derby.

"You're always looking for that one that could win the Kentucky Derby," said McGaughey. "From the very first time when you see them as yearlings out on the farm, you're wondering: Could this be the one?"

While owners and trainers may anticipate the first Saturday in May for a couple of years, during Derby Week, the frenzy sets in for everyone.

SUNNY'S HALO
THE KENTUCKY DERBY, 1983

In the spring of 1983, it rained every day for weeks in Louisville, right up to—and including—Derby Day.

Trainer David Cross was the boss of a one-horse stable: a fast colt named Sunny's Halo. Cross had given up all the other horses he was training in Toronto, and taken his star to California that winter, where it rained and rained. To find drier weather for his horse, the trainer and his wife picked up and moved again, to Arkansas. In Hot Springs, the weather was better, and Sunny's Halo prospered, culminating his stay with a victory in the Arkansas Derby.

Then Cross and Sunny's Halo vanned to Kentucky to train for the Derby. But the rains found them again.

Despite the rain, the Churchill Downs track stayed solid for training, and again Sunny's Halo did well. But with one week to go, Cross needed just a break in the daily downpour to get in one last important workout.

On Sunday morning, six days before the Derby, Cross was at the barn at 3 A.M., watching the weather. At about five, still long before sun-up, it was still pouring, but Cross got Sunny's Halo ready, saddling the colt and then walking him round and round the barn. At six o'clock, when there was just a bit of glow of sunlight in the eastern sky, a hole opened up in the clouds, and for one brief moment, it stopped raining at Churchill Downs.

The horse was ready, and Cross sent Sunny's Halo and rider Eddie Delahoussaye to the track immediately for that all-important work. The colt was big and strong—and

ready—tired of cabin fever, no doubt. Around the track Sunny's Halo zipped, coming to the finish line just as the rains began again.

But Cross had found his hole in the clouds. Back at the barn, the horse was walked, then cleaned up. As Sunny's Halo was led back into his stall, Cross closed the stall door behind the horse and fastened the catch.

"That's it," Cross announced with finality. "He's ready for the Derby."

M

ost thorough-
breds enjoy the kind attentions of their
handlers and respond well to the touch of
humans. In their earliest days at the farm,
horses are petted and handled by humans
every day, becoming prepared for a future
working relationship with people.

One of the Deans of Derby Week is a man who has nothing to do with the horse business. He's radio broadcaster Wayne Perkey, who since 1971 has gone on location every Derby Week to originate his morning drive-time radio show from the backside. Perkey's station is WHAS-84, a 50,000-watt AM station that was the first to broadcast the Kentucky Derby, back in 1925.

Over the years, anybody and everybody has dropped in for a few minutes of chat on Perkey's show.

"There are so many exciting moments, and some that were funny," said Perkey. "One year there was that guy who came from way out west with a horse called One Eyed Tom. The horse had never even been in a horse race but this guy had nominated him and brought him all the way to Kentucky to run in the Derby.

"The stewards set up a special test for the horse, to see if he could run all right. They started him out of the starting gate one morning and we had it on radio. When the horse broke out of the starting gate he took about two forward steps and then just turned to the left. The jockey had a hard time keeping One Eyed Tom from running right into the rail."

Of course, that was the end of One Eyed Tom's Derby Dream.

• • •

Each Derby Week morning begins in darkness, turns next a foggy gray, then quickly becomes brilliant in color as the sun jumps up in the sky and warms everyone. Jackets are stashed, barn swallows chatter incessantly, the lunch wagon roams the barn area with coffee and snacks, and horses come and go everywhere. All forty-seven barns are busy places, but the press is

A HISTORICAL HANDICAPPING NOTE
THE FIRST KENTUCKY DERBY

The 1875 Derby was won by Aristides, who was a little-known stablemate of a "big" horse called Chesapeake. All the wise bettors had seen Chesapeake winning races, and they stuck on him. They had little knowledge of Aristides.

But as the race unfolded, the unheralded stablemate went to the top, and stayed there. Chesapeake didn't fire, and as the field came to the top of the stretch, Hal Price McGrath, owner of both horses, found himself with just one chance. According to lore, the jock on Aristides, Oliver Lewis, knew that the stable expected his horse to be only a pacesetter for Chesapeake. Lewis looked over to McGrath for instructions as he led the field turning into the home stretch. McGrath windmilled his hat in signal, yelling to Lewis, "Go on!"

The victory was no fluke, with Aristides' time of 2:37 3/4 establishing a new American record for the 1-1/2-mile distance. (In 1896 the Derby distance was changed to 1 1/4 miles.)

An unknown writer penned this description of Aristides: "Just a little golden-red chestnut, standing fifteen hands one and three quarter inches, with a white star on his forehead and white stockinged hind legs." That's most of what we know about the winner of the first Kentucky Derby. Sounds like a very ordinary-looking horse. But in that description there is a handy lesson.

It's a good guess that Chesapeake was a larger, flashier animal, and commanded the eye of beholders. But the Derby is often won by less-conspicuous types. And smaller isn't necessarily bad. Northern Dancer, a tiny Canadian flash who appeared in 1964, set the Derby and track record for the mile-and-a-quarter and went on to sire generations of racehorses over the next twenty years. Like with humans, big, strong runners often make the best sprinters, while slighter, smaller men and women excel in marathons. The betting eye is usually with the biggest horses—even though those might not be best suited to the distance.

Bettors also love to back the horses who have won most recently. But those Derby prep races are shorter than the Derby itself, and when the distance lengthens, a new winner often emerges. The Kentucky Derby is the longest race the contenders will have ever run to that date, and it places an unusual premium on stamina, as well as speed. You sometimes need to look for a new dimension to find the winner.

Betting window sign

One morning at Gulfstream
Park, a couple of race fans were lamenting
that they couldn't get close enough to hear
what some trainers were saying as they
watched their horses work.

"If they only knew," said writer
Jack Will. "It was Rusty Arnold and Shug
McGaughey and those guys from Lexington.
They're out there on that stand every
morning all winter long, and they only talk
about one thing: University of Kentucky
basketball."

clustered mostly at barns 41 and 42, the Derby barns, huddling around the Derby horse trainers, who are fielding questions.

And the scene has always had its characters.

There is famed trainer Laz Barrera, skip-talking along in happy Cuban-English while splashing cool alcohol on his Derby horse's back and patting the liquid into its hide. Laz spins stories of how he got started years ago at the old Oriental racetrack in Havana. Nobody cares if the stories are slightly exaggerated. D. Wayne Lukas can spin a yarn, too. And Bob Baffert has everyone laughing. Minutes after working a Derby contender, jockey Pat Day holds court, delivering precise verbs and colorful nouns that detail exactly how the horse got over the track.

"The backside is such an attractive and alluring setting," explained John Asher, who is the Churchill Downs Director of News and Information. "It's such a great place for conversation, so rich with great characters and personalities. And that combination is just magical. It's the magnificent animals, and world-class riders and trainers preparing for the Derby. When you get around a big event like the Derby, there is just so much electricity. The air fairly crackles. The anticipation is so thick you can cut it."

It is that atmosphere that brings the writers and media people back year after year. And the stories they produce from those mornings fill the imaginations of readers.

"You can just feel a crescendo toward Derby Day," said Asher. "*Especially* if there's a horse that's a little bit special."

Traffic sign from Hamburg Place farm, where six Derby winners were foaled

Horse racing is an intricate sport, with many people contributing to its continued popularity. The Kentucky Racing Commission is recognized nationally as a pace-setter in the enhancement of horseracing, and is entrusted by the people of Kentucky with the preservation of a unique treasure, the Kentucky Derby.

KENTUCKY RACING COMMISSION
CHURCHILL DOWNS, 1998

The Kentucky Racing Commission is: (front row from left) Commissioner C. Frank Shoop, Chairman Richard "Smitty" Taylor, Commissioners Frank L. Jones, Jr., and V. L. Fisher Jr., M.D.; (back row from left) Executive Director/Chief Steward Bernard J. Hettel, Commissioners Richard B. Klein, Robert G. Stallings, C. Bruce Hundley, and Nathan Sholar; (not pictured) Vice Chairman John T. L. Jones, Jr., Commissioners Lon E. Fields, Sr., and Wayne E. Carlisle.

Expert hands guide the racehorse through the saddling routine in the paddock. It's an time-honored ritual in which the owners, trainers, jockeys, and horses all meet up before the race for the saddling of the horse. The principals confer and wish each other luck. Everyone except the horse finds this a very natural sequence. Horses don't socialize. They want to get on with it. Get out there and run. Some horses can't take this tedious waiting and will "lose it" to nervousness in the paddock. That's why soothing, confident hands are essential.

Exercise and racing saddles

The rider "shows the whip" to the horse he's working. The exercise rider is essentially a training jockey, teaching the horse the ropes, and helping it stay in top condition. In skilled hands, the whip is not an instrument of punishment, but rather a part of the communication equipment employed by rider and horse.

PICKING WINNERS
THE KENTUCKY DERBY

Identification badge

Thousands of words have been written and said on the subject of picking the Derby winner. But the fact is, no one knows exactly how to do it.

There seem to be, however, certain traits that nearly all Derby winners have in common: ability, foundation, peaking, pedigree. And then there is the old crystal ball.

The first thing to do in any race is narrow the field to the horses who have the ability to win. In one respect, that actually might be easier with the Kentucky Derby, because so much is known about the contenders. The horses who have run well in the big preps are the ones to beat in the Kentucky Derby. Look for horses who were running well late in those races and who have been in the battle and kept running. Fantastic runaway triumphs are often aberrations. Be wary of hype.

In a century and a quarter of Kentucky Derby history, nearly everything has happened. But one thing that has happened only once in Kentucky Derby history is that a horse who did not race at two won the Derby when he was three. Since it's been 116 years since Apollo did it, you have to figure there must be something horses get when they race at two that they need when they attempt to win the Kentucky Derby at three. So put a line through the lightly raced latecomers.

In the thinking of top trainers, preparing for the Derby is a long, continuous process from the day the horses are born, to planting seeds at two, to everything flowering on Derby Day. The final weeks leading up to the Derby are critical, and often some horses who gained a solid foundation at two, but have not been at the very top of their class, catch up and pass the early stars. Be especially alert for the "contenders" who train up a storm at the Downs coming into the Derby. They are the ones who are, as Joe Hirsch might say, "blooming on the ancient Downs."

Conversely, avoid a horse who experiences a setback in training due to a slight injury or illness close to the race. The Derby is such a supreme test that those with problems seldom win. On the backside, the hardboots say, "There can't be a straw in your path."

The Derby is part preparation, part rising to the occasion, and part capturing the magic of the moment. But many horses have had all that, only to be stopped cold by the long Derby distance.

And that distance problem was probably fore-ordained long before the horse was born. The ability to handle the 1 1/4 miles of the Kentucky Derby seems to have everything to do with pedigree—the genetic ingredients passed on in the heritage of the bloodlines.

"It doesn't matter who rides them, it doesn't matter who trains them, and it certainly doesn't matter who owns them," said Olin Gentry, who planned the matings that resulted in five Kentucky Derby winners. "In the final reckoning, they will only go as fast and as far as they were bred to go."

Sharp public handicapper Rick Cushing of The Louisville Courier-Journal buys that idea.

"The reason the Derby is so difficult to handicap is the unknown factor of distance," said Cushing. "That's why breeding is so important. It's the best clue to whether a horse can get the distance."

Pedigree is a foreign concept for most people. Breeding is a process of planned marriages, not a mixer where stallions and broodmares meet, fall in love, and have children. And of these marriages, only a few will produce a horse that will excel at the distance of a mile and a quarter.

Finally, there is the crystal ball. Experienced handicappers try to imagine how the race will be run, concentrating on the contenders and blending Derby facts with Derby magic to divine the winner. But inexperienced handicappers can use the crystal ball too.

"I try to look for the story," said Bill Wilson, who is not a racetrack regular, but gets a line on the Derby contenders in the sports pages—with a particular eye to the storylines behind the horses. Especially strong, said Wilson, are older owners, who have been looking all their lives for the Derby win. He noted Mrs. Frances Genter (who owned Unbridled), Cal Partee (Lil E. Tee), and Paul Mellon and MacK Miller (Sea Hero). "It seems like those people have been in it for so long, and they deserve to get their Derby win," explained Wilson.

There is no one certain way to pick a Derby horse. Any way that picks the winner is perfect. The thing to remember is that whatever method you use to pick your Derby horse, don't let anyone talk you out of it. Get your Derby horse, and stick to it.

Writers can find a wealth of interesting anecdotes to make the Derby such a colorful event to write about.

Cassaleria, a respected contender one year, had to be stabled in an outdoor pen. His trainer, Ron McAnally, said the horse couldn't be in a stall because he had claustrophobia. The horse also had only one good eye. And Sea Cadet, another McAnally horse, had no tail, sparking an extensive discussion about how hard it was for a tailess horse to keep its balance while running.

Then there was the guy who brought a horse to the Derby who was plainly out-classed. But the guy didn't care. He'd heard that Churchill Downs provided finish line box seats for the owners of Derby horses, and so he went around all the bars in Louisville's South End selling shares in his "Derby Horse"—with which, of course, went box seats to the Derby!

Jack Price always claimed that he didn't think the Derby was such a big deal. The trainer of 1961 Derby favorite, Carry Back, told reporters, "The Derby is just another horse race." But years later, when the Kentucky Derby Museum opened, Price had Carry Back dug up and reinterred in the museum's courtyard.

"The Kentucky Derby is a different dimension. You've always got to remember that nobody has a chance to practice at this distance. You cannot duplicate the situation. . . . It's uncharted water. That's what makes it so enormously intriguing."

—D. WAYNE LUKAS, TRAINER

Derby Day dawns early for everyone. Even before first light, workers at the track scurry around getting ready for another Kentucky Derby at venerable Churchill Downs. By afternoon, 140,000 people will be on the grounds.

Fans wake up early, too, getting ready for the big day. In homes and hotels across Louisville, and in neighboring cities in Kentucky and Southern Indiana, the first order of business is likely to be breakfast.

THE FIRST SATURDAY IN MAY

Some places will serve fancy crepes with fresh fruit and mimosas. Many folks will go for bacon and eggs, with toast and hash browns to counter the lingering effects of festive Derby Eve parties.

But people can't linger over breakfast and leisurely read the Derby Day edition of *The Louisville Courier-Journal*. There are errands: The cleaners, the tickets, the kids—and a trip to the money machine. (And don't you wonder how many $20 bills come out of those on Derby Day?) Serious horseplayers would like to get a good look at the Daily Racing Form before heading to the races, but just can't find the time. TVs and radios all over town are tuned to live reports from the track, which begin in the morning and go all day long. Over the years, local broadcast personalities have put in many a long day at the track on Derby Day. The faces and voices of Paul Rogers, Milton Metz, Melissa Forsythe, Fred Cowgill, Phyllis Knight, Cawood Ledford, and many others are an indelible part of the Derby Day scene.

Friends call to pass on tips garnered the previous evening and scribbled down on cocktail napkins. Some will request that a bet be placed on an early race because they're just not going to get to the track in time.

All across the city, the hum of machines and people moving about builds throughout the morning. Traffic picks up. Taxis honk

and busses whoosh. A traffic cop's whistle sounds shrill and stops pedestrians from stepping out in front of traffic. Nearer to the track, the volume of pedestrians grows, and so does the opportunity to purchase something of incalculable value, from T-shirts to tips to parking places. The sidewalk three-card monte game is alive and thriving—and after all these years, you still can't tell the marks from the shills.

The Infield fills, and gets more filled—and even more filled—as people click through the turnstiles, pass the bootleg booze inspections, and funnel through the tunnels. The green spaces on the great lawn diminish rapidly, and by noon all the elbow room is gone. The fun really starts at this point: a girl is tossed high on a blanket, Frisbees sail across reclined picnickers, who munch on carry-out fried chicken and reminisce about past attempts to garner cheers by climbing the now-relocated flag pole.

The Clubhouse box seats fill more slowly, gradually going from nearly deserted to jam-packed.

GOING TO THE DERBY!
THE INFIELD

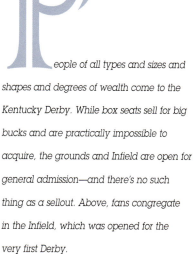

People of all types and sizes and shapes and degrees of wealth come to the Kentucky Derby. While box seats sell for big bucks and are practically impossible to acquire, the grounds and Infield are open for general admission—and there's no such thing as a sellout. Above, fans congregate in the Infield, which was opened for the very first Derby.

A 1919 complimentary ladies pass to Churchill Downs

Good Clean Fun
The Infield

There is no requirement that one must possess a carefree spirit and feel young at heart to gain admittance to the Churchill Downs Infield . . . but it helps.

While some people wouldn't think of attending the Derby unless they could count on a high-rent seat in the Clubhouse, others wouldn't dream of missing the fun of the Infield. If it's sunny, you can count on a sunburn, and if it rains, there's the mudslide.

A photographer focuses a camera before mounting it on a bracket above the inside rail of the track. These cameras are pointed up the track to capture head-on views of the stretch drive and finish. The cameras are prefocused, equipped with fast motor drives, and operated by remote control.

J WAITING
DERBY DAY

Jockeys have their own quarters and locker facilities, complete with quite a few amenities. But much of their Derby Day is spent waiting for up to an hour between races. With so much on the line in big stakes races all day on Derby Day, the waiting can be nerve-wracking.

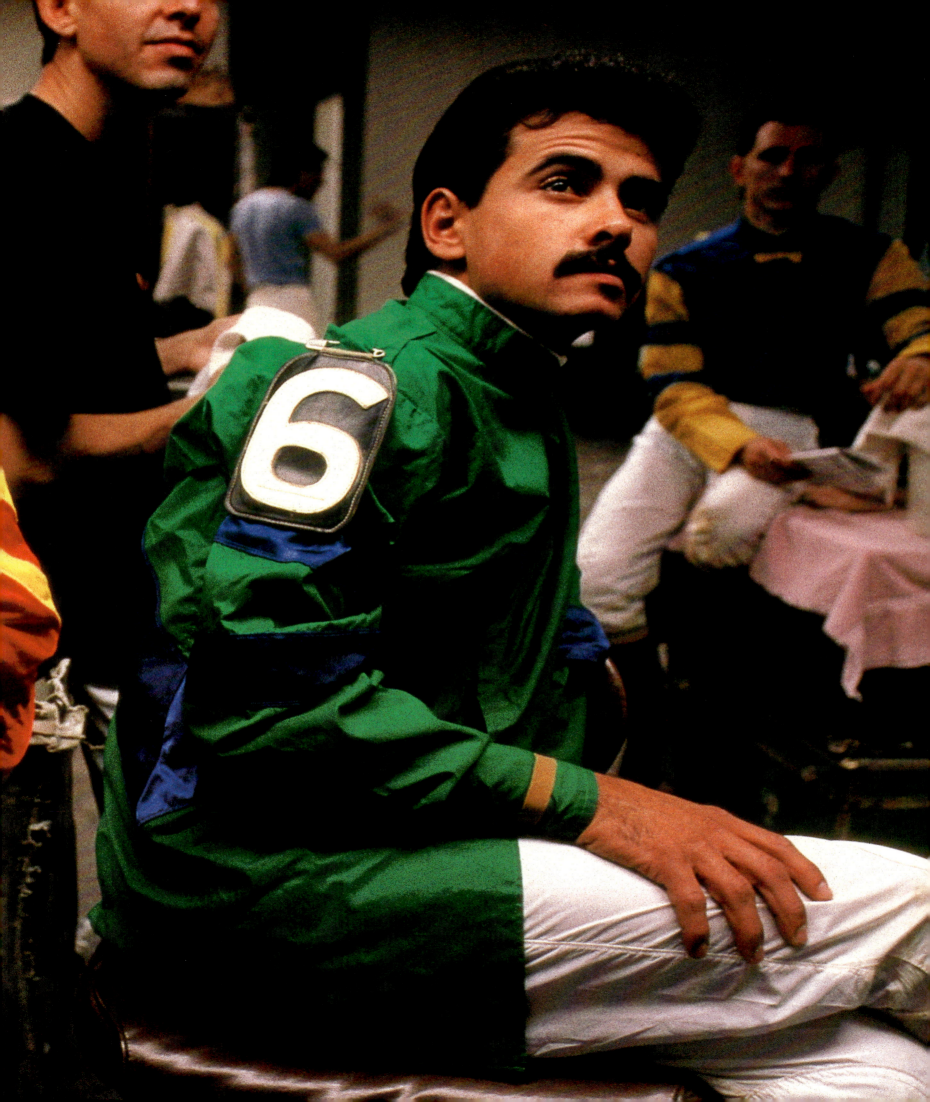

Dressed-up people wear clothes of every color, the brighter the better. That includes men's sports jackets in a shade sometimes referred to as "U.S. 60 Yellow," named for a road that brings people to Louisville from outer environs. The outfit is usually completed by plaid pants.

The first race on Derby Day goes off at 11:30, but more than half the people betting aren't betting on that race at all. They're betting the Derby, which is still hours away. Most are placing bets they've ponied to the track from friends "sending a bet out." But some people are betting the Derby at 11:30 in the morning simply because they just can't wait to get started.

And why not? What better way to start the day than with a refreshing Derby bet?

Volume picks up at the windows as the day goes on. Nowadays, there are big stakes races all day Derby Day that are very attractive for betting. Money pours into the wagering pools not only from the folks at Churchill Downs but from betting outlets throughout North America and the world, where horseplayers can play the Churchill races. Horseplayers love to bet big stakes races that feature nationally known horses. The fields are very competitive, and the wagering pools are huge.

There are, in fact, many legends and tales of bets won and lost on Derby Day and Oaks Day. On those days, when there is so much money being wagered, high rollers can bet with both hands. They don't have to worry about their bets "tilting the board," as might happen on an ordinary day, when a big bet would severely skew the odds—not to mention attract unwanted attention to a horse that is "well intended."

One Derby Day—back before the tote machines were computerized—a guy walked up to a $50 window and told the selling clerk he planned to bet $10,000 on the next race.

"That's fine," said the clerk. "Come right back here to bet. We'll be ready for you."

And they were. When the man returned he opened a

Media credential badge

PHOTO OP
THE KENTUCKY DERBY

he Derby is the photo opportunity of a lifetime, drawing professional photographers from all over the world. Nonprofessional shutterbugs also are armed with cameras, taking advantage of the presence of sleek mahogany racehorses and 140,000 interesting human subjects.

CELEBRITIES
DERBY DAY

My first Derby was in 1941, when Whirlaway won," recalled Edna Yarmuth, daughter of famed Derby hosts Sam and Hattie Klein. "It was just something you couldn't believe. There was no television then, but you would see all the pictures of the celebrities in the newspapers. Then, here we were with all those people, and all that commotion. The movie stars would parade by, and everyone would crane their necks to get a glimpse of them. The most beautiful of all was Lana Turner, wearing a turban. She was just gorgeous."

THE BIG EVENT
DERBY DAY

Adding to the atmosphere of excitment and anticipation is the perennial presence of celebrities at Churchill Downs on Derby Day. Clockwise from top: "Babe" Ruth and Louisville Slugger maker John "Bud" Hillerich; Daryl Hannah and Phyllis George Brown; Bob Hope and his wife, Delores; Muhammed Ali; and Jack Nicholson.

briefcase and chucked out $10,000 in wrapped bills. The mutuels manager counted the money while the clerk punched out $10,000 worth of $50 win tickets on the horse—two hundred tickets.

They ran the race, and the horse won. He went off at 3-1, so the guy was due to collect $40 grand. When he returned to the window, they were all ready for him.

"Congratulations," said the mutuels manager, as he verified the winning tickets. "Would you like a check for the $40,000?"

The guy just opened up the lid on his briefcase and said, "Did I bet with a check?"

Betting is part of the excitement of Derby Day. And bettors don't have to tote $40,000 away from the window to have a good time. Fans who cheer home winners on which they've wagered no more than $2 break out into grins when they step into the "smiling line" after a race to collect.

Derby Day is full of pageantry, from post parades and bright-colored silks to the clarion blare of the bugle sounding the "call to post." The University of Louisville band and the Fort Knox Army band perform, and the crowd lets out whoops and pleas when the horses run. The race-caller's singsong cadence gives a rhythm to the races. Track concessionaires sell countless juleps

and soft drinks and hot dogs, while a slew of drumsticks are carried onto the grounds in buckets of Kentucky Fried Chicken. Colonel Sanders is definitely the number-one carry-in at Churchill Downs, which is appropriate for a place that abounds with genuine Kentucky Colonels.

The Kentucky Derby is everybody's race. It belongs to no one and to one and all. It might have been best described in that old oft-quoted line by Kentucky-born humorist Irvin S. Cobb, that goes, "Until you've been to Kentucky, and with your own eyes beheld a Kentucky Derby, you ain't never been nowhere, and you ain't never seen nothing." Derby goers and Derby fans around the world know this to be true.

But all that happens leading up to the Derby is just build-up for when the Derby is finally run.

The Derby is officially on when the previous race, the Early Times Turf Classic, is run and the "OFFICIAL" sign lights on the tote board. At that moment, from one end of

PRELUDE TO THE BIG EVENT
CHURCHILL DOWNS

*M*uch goes on before the Derby horses set hoof on the track. Above: Kentucky Derby winner Unbridled, with jockey Craig Perret aboard, makes his way around a crowded Churchill Downs paddock before the Parade to Post for the 1990 Derby.

Left: Inside the famed dirt oval that hosts the Kentucky Derby is the Matt Winn Turf Course, site of other important stakes races run on Derby Day and throughout the race season.

1899 Louisville Jockey Club Stable pass

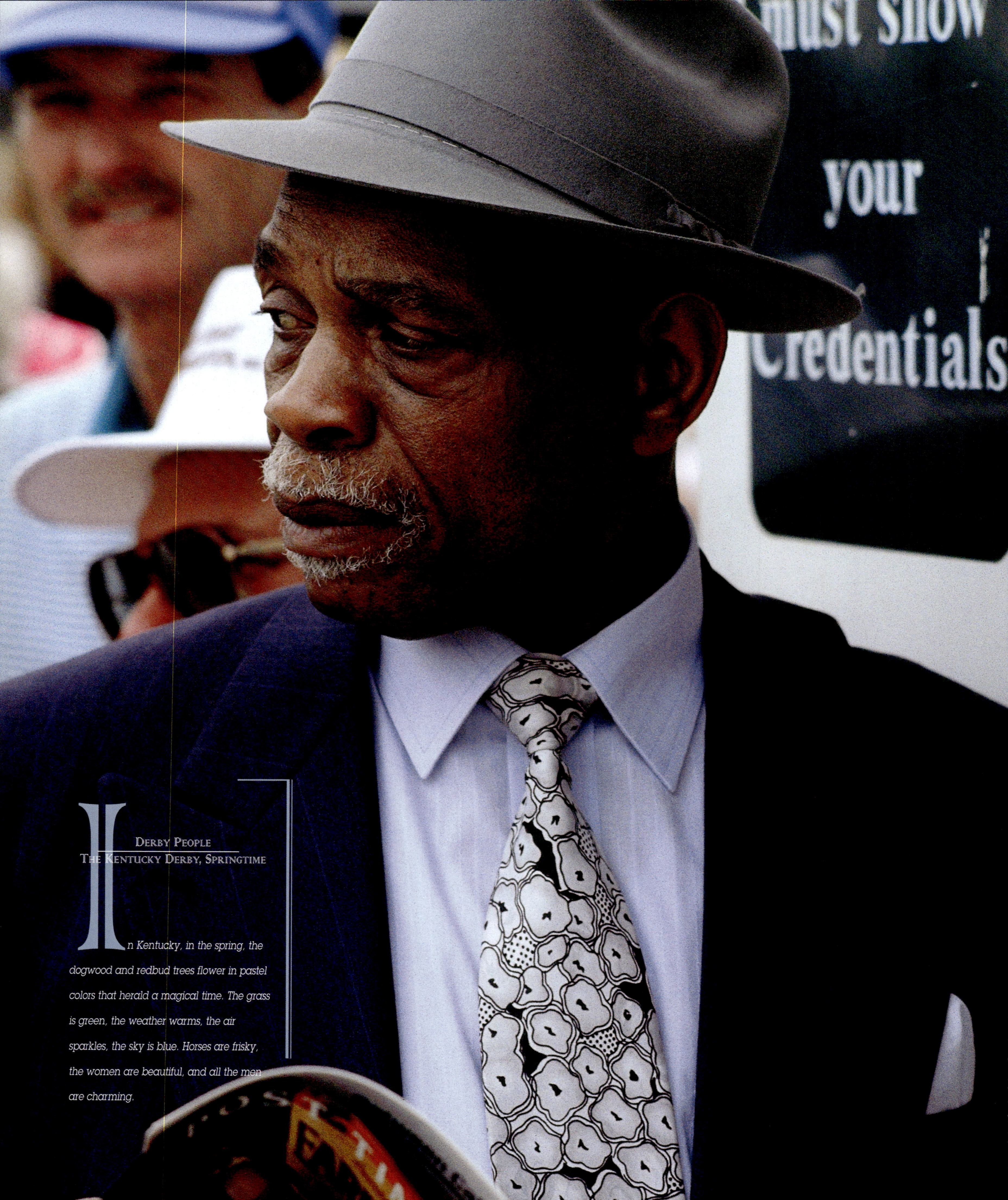

must show
your
Credentials

Derby People
The Kentucky Derby, Springtime

In Kentucky, in the spring, the dogwood and redbud trees flower in pastel colors that herald a magical time. The grass is green, the weather warms, the air sparkles, the sky is blue. Horses are frisky, the women are beautiful, and all the men are charming.

the track to the other, every pari-mutuel betting machine makes a little sound and the world of wagering is rebooted: ready for business. It's not really an organized cheer that goes up from the huge throng, but it does seem as if everyone senses that the time has arrived for the great show. All in attendance get just the first flicker of a butterfly in the stomach because there is nothing left but the climax: One hour to post time for the Kentucky Derby!

• • •

Over in the barn area, there are a few minutes of waiting (after an eternity of all-day waiting), and then the call comes on the barn area loudspeaker announcing to the horse people that it is time to, "Bring 'em over for the Kentucky Derby."

This is a wonderful moment of the Derby, when grooms snap on lead shanks and lead their horses out of their stalls. Through the crowded barn area and up through a "gap" in the backstretch fence, the contenders

LORD DERBY
THE KENTUCKY DERBY, 1930

The first Kentucky Derby to be seen by a real "Derby" came in 1930, when Lord Derby traveled from England to Kentucky to see the American version of the race named for his ancestor. It was the twelfth Lord Derby who had helped found the Derby at Epsom, after which the Kentucky Derby was modeled. The seventeenth Lord Derby (right) was a big hit in Louisville, and gave terrific interviews. He viewed the race from a special stand built for him, and joined in the winner's circle celebration after the race with Gallant Fox and his owner William Woodward. "I came 5,000 miles to see this Derby," he said, graciously. "I was pleased to see a good horse win."

Lord Derby also straightened everyone out on the pronunciation of the word derby, whether it was pronounced durby or darby. "Both are correct," he said, "but the hat's a bowler."

for the race—and all their official retinue of people—come onto the track for the long walk over to the grandstand for the Kentucky Derby. All those with a view crane their necks to see the horses and people "come over" to be saddled for the Derby.

The horse parade comes around the Clubhouse turn, then up the stretch past the finish line and under the Twin Spires, passing beneath the grandstand to the paddock, where they are saddled for the Kentucky Derby.

The paddock is packed with owners, trainers, grooms, friends, newspeople, and officials. Each horse is identified by a judge who checks its lip tattoo and physical characteristics to see that it is, indeed, the right horse. It is a chaotic scene of people and horses. But most know the routine well, and somehow it is accomplished in about ten minutes. The jockeys come down the stairs from the jocks' room and shake hands with the

Souvenir leather program cover presented to Lord Derby

Whisky flask commemorating Lord Derby's visit

ON YOUR TOES
DERBY DAY AT CHURCHILL DOWNS

IF *ancy footwear is always in style at the Derby, whether adorning an expensive outfit on Millionaires Row, or striding across the bricks of the first floor grounds. After a day on their feet, some fans concede to comfort over chic.*

owners. Then the riders huddle with the trainers for a few last-minute words. They've gone over the tactics to be employed already, but the trainer might still say something like, "Try to get him to relax the first time down the stretch past the stands," and, "Good luck."

"Riders up," booms the voice of the paddock judge. The trainers give a leg up to the riders and send them back out through the tunnel and onto the world's most famous track as the University of Louisville band strikes up Stephen Foster's "My Old Kentucky Home."

The crowd sings along as best it can through the opening verse—few know those words exactly—then chimes in loud and clear with the chorus, "Weep no more my lady . . ." And 70,000 ladies weep. (Some men do, too.)

The song lasts just the length of the post parade, and as they, "sing one song for My Old Kentucky Home, far away," a tremendous cheer rolls up from the crowd. The Derby is ON!

The horses break from their walk in the post parade into a slow canter, and make their way up the track, up the stretch in front of the grandstand, as thousands continue cheering. They go past where the race will start, and up around the far turn. Ten minutes later they have turned and headed back to the starting gate to load for the race.

THIS is the place and the time—awaited for one entire year—when the crowd stands on tiptoes, and millions of viewers lean closer to their television screens, as the field of horses are led to the starting gate. The Starter watches everything closely, barking commands to his skilled staff of assistant starters. These starters safely guide as many as twenty skittish thoroughbreds into their appointed stalls, hop onto ledges on the sides of the stalls, and steady the horses' heads before the gate springs open. The starting staff is aware of the individual idiosyncracies of each horse, and there is a starter with each runner, ready to perform the necessary duties to get the horse into the stall and ready for the start.

In one minute, every horse will be loaded and ready. Every jockey set. Every fan on the brink of show time. Everything we know about this remarkable piece of Americana is concentrated into a long line of starting gate stalls, waiting to explode. . . .

And what must the horse be thinking?

GETAHUNCH BETABUNCH
THE KENTUCKY DERBY

Mud slides, mint juleps, blanket tosses—that's all fun, but the serious business of Derby Day is picking winners. And the art of betting the ponies has certainly inspired all sorts of wit and wisdom. Such as this sound advice: "Bet light on the losers, and heavy on the winners." Or "Getahunch betabunch."

(Racing pundit Mike Barry always noted that, "When they say 'Getahunch betabunch,' they neglect to add, 'and all next week you'll eat no lunch.'")

And how about this one, from the mind of a guy named Pebbles, who says, "The less you bet, the more you lose when you win."

MEMORIES
THE KENTUCKY DERBY, 1963

My dad, Bill Sr., took my sister Jean and me to the 1963 Kentucky Derby. We stuck close to him as he led us through the turnstiles and ahead into the tunnel under the track. It was packed with people, and got more packed as we descended under the track. The college kids mooed like cattle driven by cowboys. They laughed at each other's moos. We mooed, too.

Then it was out of the tunnel darkness and into the brilliant sunshine of the Infield at Churchill Downs. And right at the very top of the tunnel, on our first step into the Infield was a guy in an old-fashioned hat, standing on a wooden stand and barking, "Dan Carter. Dan Carter. Get your winners from Dan Carter."

It was an amazing display. I'd never seen anybody like this guy before. Tucked into his hatband was a copy of the gray "tip-sheet" he was hawking. It had a picture of a guy wearing a hat. If you know trainer Harvey Vanier, with his patented old-fashioned brimmed hat, that was what Dan Carter's picture looked like. Just like Harvey Vanier. And it was that picture on the card that proved this guy was THE genuine Dan Carter. (Who would accept an imitation?)

Some wise guy asked, "Are you THE Dan Carter?"

"Yes I am, son," Dan replied. "That's my picture right here on the card—the card with all the winners on it."

"Well, what are you doing in here?"

"You mean, how come I'm here in the infield, instead of over with the big shots? Well, I've got other guys selling Dan Carter's picks over there, but I started out here, and this is where I like to be every Derby Day."

The wise guy didn't buy a card, but I wanted to.

My dad explained that if Dan really knew who was going to win, he wouldn't have to sell everybody the tip sheets. He'd just bet on the winners.

The other reason we didn't need Dan Carter's card was that I, personally, knew who would win the Kentucky Derby. I was, by then, a Derby Expert, and I knew the winner would be Never Bend.

Naturally, I was wrong. Never Bend was a strong pick, all right: the second choice in the betting at 3-1. And he was the smart choice of the wise newspapermen who covered the Derby. But Never Bend ran third. The winner was Chateaugay, and he paid off at a big price. Ever since that day, I am very cautious about favorites in the Kentucky Derby.

We stood on a concrete bench on tiptoes as the Derby was run, and we could see a little bit. For most of the race, we knew the horses were running, but they were out of sight. Finally, around the turn for home, they flashed by in speeding little bits of colors.

The dark coats of the horses, and the bright silks of the jockeys—just flying glimpses, flickering images seen between people who lined the infield fence. That's all we could see. But it was enough.

In his tip sheet, *above left*, analyst Tod picked several winners on the 1965 Derby Day card, including Derby winner Lucky Debonair.
The familiar-looking hat and powerful binoculars, *left*, were part of the wardrobe for two-time Derby-winning trainer Woody Stephens.

K

eyed-up Derby horses roar out of the starting gate in the 1987

Kentucky Derby. But all that rage to run is carefully held in check by the hands of masterful

riders who look for tactical position and hope to save their mount's big run for later.

The jockeys of the six inside starters pictured (of a field of seventeen) have a

combined total of more than 30,000 victories.

From the right are Jose Santos (on Cryptoclearance), Herb McCauley (on War),

Chris McCarron (in blue and white blocks on Alysheba, the eventual winner), Greg Hutton

(on Templar Hill), Angel Cordero, Jr. (on Capote), and Bill Shoemaker (on Gulch).

No horse has ever been in this kind of supercharged atmosphere. As the Derby horse stands in the narrow stall of the starting gate, its sides nearly touch the gate walls. Its nose is on the front gate, and the back door is slammed shut.

Boxed!

The horse knows the gate will spring open any second. The adrenaline, already flowing a mile a minute though its bloodstream, surges at an even faster pace. The legs quiver. Some feet dance a bit, nervously. But most of the horses try to get their feet planted and knees bent, ready to surge forward at the moment the gate opens.

And what does the horse see?

Not very much. A horse's eyes are on the side of its head, and it can see best the things closest to it—like the horse next to it in the gate. Ahead is a long, wide-open path of tan, sandy racetrack, with harrow lines rolling straight away into the horizon. The horse will follow those lines if it can and try to run in a straight line. But mostly, it cannot see very far ahead. It certainly cannot see the end of the long stretch, one-quarter of a mile away. But that may not matter. Horses run on instinct, not to a surveyor's point.

BANG! The stalls of the starting gate slam open, and a bell rings its alarm.

The horse LUNGES forward into the first step of its stride, immediately blasting away from the gate and into the open. All the competitors charge forward, almost all in perfect unison. The jocks hang onto their horses' manes to keep from being thrown off in the violent first stride, and to maintain their balance when these 1,000 lbs. athletes bang into each other coming away from the gate. Holding the mane doesn't bother the horse at all. It knows riders. But what it does not know is what is about to happen even before it plants its feet to make the second stride: 50,000 people on its left side and 90,000 on its right all shout at once:

"THEY'RE OFF!"

GOGGLES
CHURCHILL DOWNS

Goggles protect a jock's eyes from dirt thrown back by the hooves in front. When the track is very wet, a jock may stack six or seven pairs of goggles to cover his or her eyes, peeling off a pair at a time and pulling them down under the chin as they become covered with mud.

Bill Shoemaker autographed this pair of goggles, that is now housed in the Kentucky Derby Museum collection.

THE HAT PARADE
DERBY DAY

Special Derby hats are a Derby tradition, but no one knows just why. WHAS-television personality Phyllis Knight probably had as much to do with fostering the tradition as anyone. Knight always made a point to talk to people on the air about the hats that crowned their Derby outfits. Of course, not all Derby hats are elegant. There are no rules of taste or limits on extravgance in the annual Derby Hat Parade.

It's a tremendous cheer in unison, but with that blast of sound, the world of fans, and reporters, and juleps, and trifectas and new dresses is all finished. Now, it's all up to horse and rider.

"I had made up my mind to get to the rail and scrape paint around the first turn," said jockey Kent Desormeaux, rider of 1998 Derby contender Real Quiet. "That was [trainer] Bob Baffert's thinking when he picked an inside post for the horse: Just get to the rail, let the speed horses go, and save horse for later."

In just 24 seconds, the field of fifteen three-year-old thoroughbreds flies a quarter mile down the stretch past the long grandstand. Owner Mike Pegram watched the race with the grooms of the horses along the track. His horse, Real Quiet, flashed by so fast that Pegram could hardly see the red and gold silks Desormeaux was wearing, or the black blinker mask and blue shadow roll on his horse's face, or the Number 2 on his saddle cloth. And, of course, horse and rider could not see him. All of those breathless, helpless, cheering, bedazzled 140,000 fans were outside the race, just a blur.

Real Quiet broke alertly, and Desormeaux was able to guide the colt over to the inside, to "scrape paint" along the rail around the first turn and into the backstretch. Real Quiet relaxed and galloped with the herd, gliding along about sixth or seventh and letting the speed horses go, just biding his time.

"I situated myself in a great relaxing spot all the way down the backside—and then the posse came," said Desormeaux. to reporters after the race. "I slid him to the outside of Indian Charlie [the race favorite], and all by himself he started progressing and moving forward."

Suddenly, those red silks over a bay horse were moving fastest of all on the outside on the turn for home.

"I'm thinking, 'Look at him go!'" said Desormeaux. "He just took off, all by himself."

Desormeaux described the changes in his emotions as Real Quiet showed him he could win the Derby.

"At the half-mile pole, and the three-eighths pole, it was, 'Well, all right.' Then when we hit this point [at the head of the homestretch] it was like, 'Oh. My God, it's now or never,' and that's when I drew my knife [whip] and went to work and got all I could."

A Piece of Derby History
The Kentucky Derby, 1875

The inscription on the tendon boots, right, reads: "This boot presented to J. M. Thornton by H.P. McGrath. Worn by Aristides 1875. Later worn by Red Cloud and Bob Forsythe."

Horses don't accumulate much "stuff." Things like blinkers and bridles and boots are generally passed along from one horse to the next in a stable. And they don't have old hats and letter sweaters. So historical artifacts to remember famous horses by are very rare, which is what is unique about these leather boots. The pads are worn on the front lower legs, protecting the tendons from being whacked by the shoes on the rear hooves when the horse is running. These were worn by Aristides when he won the first Kentucky Derby in 1875. More than a century later, when the new Kentucky Derby Museum opened, the family of Mr. Thornton presented the boots to the museum, where they are on display.

Jockey Shane Sellers receives encouragement from the fans on his way to the paddock prior to the race.

The magnificent thorough-bred racehorse, in full flight and fluid fury, and the skilled rider, steady in strength and balance, become as one as they sail to victory in the Kentucky Derby.

By the time of the Derby, the jockeys have long before proven they possess the skills, wit, and nerve needed for the big event. But the winning horse has but one chance. It must somehow sense the moment and rise to the occasion.

"Some horses are frightened by that big crowd and all that excitement," said trainer D. Wayne Lukas. "Others get their game faces on. They feed on the adrenaline."

In the final yards, Victory Gallop loomed boldly on Real Quiet's outside, cutting margin between the two with every stride. But Desormeaux kept his horse encouraged, eventually putting the whip away and just pushing forward on Real Quiet's neck, holding him together to a Kentucky Derby victory.

"When I turned for home, I asked him for his life, and he gave it to me," said Desormeaux.

And then it was over—Desormeaux standing tall in the irons, pumping his fist to the sky, the cheers of the fans becoming again a part of the drama. The horse, tired but knowing he won, returned on the turf track to the Winner's Circle.

Another Derby mystery solved. Real Quiet was given a chance, but he was not exactly the horse that was supposed to win the Derby. Several others, including stablemate Indian Charlie, were given better chances. Real Quiet was an 8-1 shot in the betting. Some fancied him. More did not.

It's why, after a century and a quarter, when life has changed from the world of the horse to the world of the automobile, to the world of the future, they still run the Kentucky Derby: because no one knows who will win. It is the great mystery.

VIVA CANONERO!
THE KENTUCKY DERBY, 1971

Jockey Gustavo Avila, above, rises in triumph as Canonero II reaches the finish line first in the 1971 Derby.

Like that of Real Quiet, left, Canonero's victory was totally unexpected. The horse was shipped from Venezuela in an old plane that also carried chickens. He spent several days in quarantine in Miami, where he got no exercise. He was then vanned one thousand miles to Louisville, where he was lightly regarded—if noticed at all.

The victory was no fluke, however. After coming from far back to win the Derby, Canonero flew to the front and led all the way in the Preakness. An all-time Belmont record crowd saw Canonero miss in his bid for the Triple Crown. But the next season, Canonero further validated his Derby win when he defeated 1972 Derby winner Riva Ridge.

Churchill Downs finish line pole

Fans sqeeze right up to the fence as a crowded field of horses bends into the first turn of the 1931 Kentucky Derby. Jockey Charley Kurtsinger, who grew up in the Downs neighborhood, has eventual winner Twenty Grand tucked back in the pack at this early point. Twenty Grand, owned by the Whitney family's powerful Greentree Stable, was a popular winner. The colt broke Old Rosebud's track record and, as was the custom of the day, lent his name to commercial products from cigarettes to razor blades.

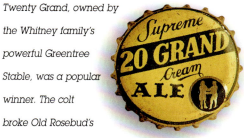

VICTORY GALLOP AND REAL QUIET
THE BELMONT STAKES, 1998

*R*eal Quiet missed becoming the twelfth Triple Crown champion in history by mere inches in 1998. After earning a Derby victory and reinforcing that feat with a snappy triumph in the Preakness, Real Quiet seemed well on his way to Triple Crown stardom when he opened up on the field in the stretch of the Belmont Stakes.

But rival Victory Gallop launched a late move that caught Real Quiet in the very last stride of the "Test of Champions." The photo showed a difference of about 6 inches at the wire.

Victory Gallop had proven a most tenacious challenger to Real Quiet throughout the Triple Crown series, twice settling for second while Real Quiet got the glory. "Our horse has run hard every time," said winning trainer Elliott Walden. "I think it's fair to turn the tables."

The Belmont Stakes finish, with Victory Gallop just winning by inches at the end of 1 1/2 miles, is a reminder of how tough a proposition the Triple Crown series is: Three very long races for very young horses, packed into a five-week period at three different racetracks.

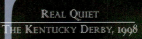

Jockey Kent Desormeaux pumps his fist in triumph after guiding the lightly considered Real Quiet to a 1998 Kentucky Derby victory.

"When I turned for home, I asked him for his life, and he gave it to me," Desormeaux said.

THE FIGHTING FINISH
THE KENTUCKY DERBY, 1933

Jockeys Herb Fisher on Head Play
(left) and Don Meade on Broker's Tip.
Taken in 1933 by The Louisville Courier-
Journal photographer Wallace Lowry, this
photograph captures Meade and Fisher
grabbing saddles and slashing at each
other with their whips as they neared
the wire.

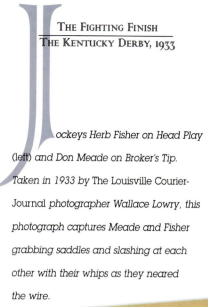

On the fiftieth anniversary of their
infamous "Fighting Finish," jockeys Don Meade
(left) and Herb Fisher (right) were reunited for a
more civil portrait. In 1933, both jockeys
received long suspensions for
what was considered equal
fault on each of their
parts, and Meade's
victory aboard
Broker's Tip was
allowed to stand.

Though he has ridden in
many Derbies now, and has won the 1992
renewal, champion jockey Pat Day still gets
the same goosebumps he got the first time he
came onto the track with a horse for the
Kentucky Derby.

"It happened on the first Saturday
in May in 1982 when I rode my first
Kentucky Derby," recalled Day. "I was on a
horse trained by Tommy Morgan called
Music Leader. As we rode out onto the racetrack that afternoon with everyone singing
'My Old Kentucky Home,' I was overcome by
emotion. I had big tears in my eyes and a
lump in my throat. It was the moment, the
atmosphere, the history, and everything
about that first Kentucky Derby."

Romance and classic rivalries are what the Kentucky Derby is all about: Swaps and Nashua; Easy Goer and Sunday Silence; Bill Shoemaker and Bill Hartack; Calumet, Claiborne, and a winner from out of the blue.

It was Derby Day of the year in which Affirmed and Alydar came to a showdown at Churchill Downs in one of the sport's greatest stories. *The Louisville Courier-Journal*'s page-one layout was all the Derby. There was a photo of Affirmed, turning for home in the Santa Anita Derby, red coat bathed in the late-afternoon sunshine. There was a picture of Alydar, bent regally munching a clump of clover—the perfect horse from countless generations of perfect thoroughbred matings—representing fabled Calumet Farm. And there was a picture of a seventeen-year-old jockey who had become, in just one year, the riding sensation of racing. That was Steve Cauthen, The Kid.

HEROES AND LEGENDS

The lead story was written by *Courier* ace Billy Reed. The photos were credited. But there was no acknowledgment of just who it was in the newsroom who composed the headline that summed up what was about to happen on that First Saturday in May in 1978. That anonymous headline writer got it all just right, crafting a headline that read: "The 104th: Romance, and a Classic Rivalry."

PENNY CHENERY TWEEDY
THE KENTUCKY DERBY, 1972 AND 1973

The Derby victory of Secretariat, and the one the previous year with Riva Ridge, capped a great hope of owner Penny Chenery Tweedy, who became a hero of sports fans with her gracious and charming personality.

"You see, I didn't grow up with horse racing, exactly," said Tweedy. "I lived in New York and rode horses, but my dad, Chris Chenery, was the one with the racehorses, at the tracks, and on the farm in Virginia. That was Meadow Stud. It was his great ambition to win the Kentucky Derby. Three times he had been favored, but not won.

"When Dad got sick and was very ill, I took over the stable, more to run it for him, than anything," said Tweedy. "Then when Riva Ridge won the Derby, we called Dad and a nurse told him the news. She thought he did understand that he had finally won the Derby."

With the same team intact, Tweedy, jockey Turcotte, and trainer Lucien Laurin returned to Louisville the following year with Secretariat. Today those team members remain wonderful ambassadors of thoroughbred racing.

SECRETARIAT
THE KENTUCKY DERBY, 1973

Secretariat came along at a time when racing desperately needed a hero—and he was that, in spades.—Cawood Ledford, sportscaster

To his fans, Secretariat was a thoroughbred wonder. He was the stuff of dreams in the same way Willie Mays and Muhammad Ali, and Notre Dame and Babe Ruth, became bigger than life. Secretariat captured the imagination.

Racing fans were waiting for a champion, and when Secretariat came along in 1973, he did so in such a sparkling way that he became more than a champion of horse racing. He became a champion for ordinary people of all walks of life—whether they had ever seen a horse race or not.

In front of a record 134,000 fans gathered at Churchill Downs for the 99th Derby, the big red chestnut destroyed twelve opponents with a last-to-first charge in which he ran every quarter mile faster than the one previous. "In the Derby, when we came out of the gate, I just let him do what he wanted to do, and that was just let them all go, and settle in the back in a gallop," said his jockey, Ron Turcotte. "Up in the stands, they might not have liked it that much. But that's what he wanted to do. And when he was ready, he just went after those horses in his own way."

Secretariat's Derby record time of 1:59 2/5 for the 1 1/4 miles was the first ever run under two minutes, and the mark stands today. And his Triple Crown victory, capped by a remarkable performance in the Belmont Stakes, became the first since Citation's in 1948— twenty-five years previous.

Even more remarkable than his list of accomplishments was the way Secretariat thoroughly energized the sport of horse racing. No wonder 163,628 fans were on hand the following year for the 100th running of the Kentucky Derby.

ALYDAR AND AFFIRMED
THE TRIPLE CROWN, 1978

*T*he period of the late 1970s, when Secretariat ruled and Affirmed and Alydar dueled—and champions Seattle Slew and Spectacular Bid came along, too— proved to be a Golden Age of the Derby.

A lot of that had to do with the long and storied rivalry between Alydar and Affirmed. The years were 1977 and 1978: two years in which those two horses dominated the American racing scene and produced drama the likes of which is seldom seen, but always remembered, in sport.

In the end, they raced each other many times, and Affirmed came out on top. Except in the hearts of their respective fans, where it was a tie.

It was Affirmed who won the Kentucky Derby, left, the Preakness, and the Belmont to take the Triple Crown—each time defeating Alydar. Each time by a smaller margin. Each time with drama more emotionally draining than the time before.

Alydar came along at a time when the heyday of Calumet Farm had passed. But he rekindled that old Calumet magic, and all of racing was enthralled. In a touching scene at Keeneland, right, jockey Jorge Velasquez took Alydar out of the post parade and over to the rail so that his elderly owners, Admiral (far right) and Mrs. Gene Markey (third from right) could see their star.

Affirmed had his following, as well. He too came from a great racing tradition—the Jacobs and Wolfson families—that belonged more to the common man than to the royalty of racing.

Affirmed and Alydar began their rivalry as two-year-olds in the East, and all summer long they were finishing one-two and two-one. Fans and writers were caught up in the enthralling drama. Here were two horses who were destined to duke it out, and no other horses mattered in their presence.

"What was it that made the difference between the two colts?" asked turf writer Dan Farley. "After more than nine miles of competition the superiority of one over the other could be voiced in a whisper. Still, the difference was there, and it had come from within."

STEVE CAUTHEN
THE KENTUCKY DERBY, 1978

One thing everyone liked about Affirmed was "The Kid." That was eighteen-year-old Steve Cauthen, the son of a racetrack family from Northern Kentucky. Cary Golde, who is renowned as a handicapper but has also owned a few horses, remembers Steve Cauthen at fifteen years of age.

"Stevie was the kid hanging around the barn that we'd send out to get coffee. A real nice kid. You didn't think then that someday he would be the best rider in the world, but he wanted to be a rider. We'd all be hanging around at the barn talking, and Steve would throw his legs across a bale of straw and pretend he was a jockey. He said he'd be a jockey someday."

And that day came sooner than later. Cauthen began riding for real when he turned sixteen. He was immediately the leading apprentice rider in North America, and when he was seventeen he set a world earnings record for jockeys of $6,000,000 in one season. The next year, he was aboard Affirmed, coming back to Kentucky to win the Derby.

ALYSHEBA
THE KENTUCKY DERBY, 1987

It was Alysheba who turned in perhaps the most remarkable Derby performance of all time. As the horse came hard down the lane and overtook rival Bet Twice, Alysheba's front hooves caught the rear hooves of Bet Twice. Alysheba stumbled, his head went down, and it looked like both he and jockey Chris McCarron would tumble head-over-heels. But the horse was an athlete, and McCarron hung on. Alysheba caught himself up—then got back running and still won the Derby!

A poll of writers labeled McCarron's ride one of the best of the twentieth century.

"I'm flattered, but I think the horse deserves a lot more credit than I do," said McCarron. "He clipped heels, and I thought I was a goner. All I did was hang on. He did all the work. I've never ridden a horse that showed so much courage."

Eddie Arcaro won the first of his five Kentucky Derbies in 1938, and Bill Shoemaker won the last of his four in 1986, but the careers of those two great Derby-riding heroes overlapped, and the two were always compared.

The scribes once posed the question to Shoemaker, asking whom did he think was best, himself or Arcaro.

"Arcaro is the greatest rider," said Shoemaker. So then they went to Arcaro and said, "Shoemaker says you are the best. What do you say?"

"Shoemaker's right, I'm the best," said Arcaro. "But," he added, "horses run for Shoemaker."

Which, as well as anything, tells the story of two guys who set the modern standard for race riding in America. Two guys who respected each other and were friends. And two guys who are certainly standards for riding accomplishment in the Kentucky Derby.

BILL SHOEMAKER
THE KENTUCKY DERBY, 1955, 1959, 1965, AND 1986

While Bill Shoemaker's nickname, "The Shoe," is derived from his last name, it's rather fitting since he started out life in a shoebox. When Shoemaker was delivered almost two months premature and weighing only two pounds, the doctor said that the infant would not last the night. But little Bill's grandmother placed the baby in a shoebox and set him inside the oven with the heat turned low and the door open. It made for a kind of incubator, and in the morning Bill Shoemaker was still alive. Shoemaker's family later moved to California, and the small but tough kid excelled as a high school wrestler. But when he became a jockey, Shoemaker didn't wrestle his mounts. He controlled them with his fingertips.

The Shoe was a sensation from the start. He was based in California, but rode in Chicago and New York as well.

Shoemaker won his first Derby on Swaps, in 1955, at the age of twenty-three. In 1986, when he was fifty-four, Shoemaker won his fourth Derby with Ferdinand—and they were still talking about his feather-touch hands.

Fairly or not, Shoemaker will also be remembered for a mistake he made in the famous 1957 Derby, in which he misjudged the finish line and ended up losing the race by a nose to Iron Liege. Some feel that moment's let-up a sixteenth-of-a-mile from the finish cost Gallant Man the race. Others say Gallant Man never lost his stride, and just got beaten. Either way, Shoemaker stoically took the heat.

Two years later, Shoemaker won one he could have lost, when he got Tomy Lee up to beat Sword Dancer in a stretch-long drive to the wire. "Every time I would ask Tomy Lee, he would put his head in front, but Sword Dancer would pass him right back," said Shoemaker. "So I waited for the wire, and just at the last instant, I asked Tomy Lee, and he stuck his nose out ahead. Sword Dancer passed him right back, but it was too late."

Bill Shoemaker retired as the leading rider in history with 8,833 victories.

Arcaro and Lawrin in 1938

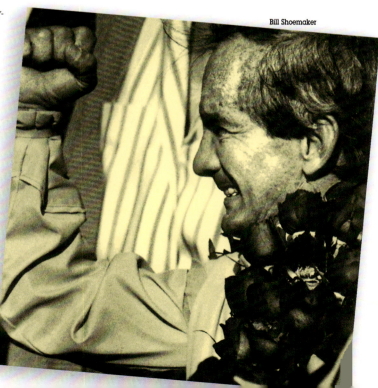

Bill Shoemaker

EDDIE ARCARO
THE KENTUCKY DERBY, 1938, 1941, 1945, 1948, AND 1952

Arcaro was the big talker, with loads of friends in all sporting venues.

"He was a people person," Joe Hirsch wrote in Arcaro's obituary in 1997. Hirsch said that when Arcaro died, "that was the first time he went anywhere unaccompanied."

Arcaro grew up in Newport, Kentucky, and moved east to become the king of New York riders. When he came up in the 1930s, riding was a tougher game, but Arcaro was equal to the challenge. He wrote a book called I Ride to Win, and there was no question that that's exactly what he did. He once drew a one-year suspension for trying to put a rival jock over the fence. But after that, he toned down his act and stuck strictly to riding. That's when they began to call him "The Master."

Arcaro's big Derby break came when he hooked up with trainer Ben Jones to win the 1938 Derby with Lawrin. When Plain Ben went to Calumet, Arcaro and Jones stuck together. In 1941, the pair hit Derby paydirt again with Whirlaway. Arcaro won three more, with Hoop Jr. in 1945, Citation (1948), and Hill Gail (1952).

Arcaro's most famous Derby ride came aboard Whirlaway, a difficult horse that needed all the genius of Jones and Arcaro to reach his potential. Arcaro won easily with Citation, whom he called the best horse he ever rode. "Like driving a Cadillac," he said.

Sometimes after an inspiring performance, people will say of a horse, "He was not to be denied." Seattle Slew's attitude toward opponents was more like, "Get the heck out of my way! Now!" Slew's trademark style was to break on the lead. But in the 1977 Kentucky Derby, he suffered an awkward start, which quickly became a problem—for the other thirteen horses. Slew unapologetically bulled his way through the field. First he slammed Get the Axe out of his way. Then he put a hip into Sir Sir. Then Slew pushed three horses—Flag Officer, Affiliate, and Bob's Dusty—to the outside. Arriving at the front of the pack, he engaged For the Moment in a duel for the lead. At the head of the stretch, he ran away from them all.

After winning the Derby, Preakness, and Belmont, Slew was the first and only undefeated Triple Crown champion. Yet he wasn't the type of horse from whom a lot was expected: He was purchased as a yearling for only $17,500. The main reason he sold so cheaply was that he wasn't much to look at.

Paul and Christine Mallory, who foaled the son of Bold Reasoning and My Charmer, agreed that Seattle Slew was somewhat "mulish." The truth, said Paul Mallory, is that "he was ugly. He had big ears, and they flopped over for the first week." But even that became part of his legend.

Today, Seattle Slew is the second oldest living Derby winner (behind Bold Forbes, 1976 winner) and remains one of the leading stallions in the world.

Seattle Slew rockets away from challengers in the Hialeah Park Flamingo Stakes, a Florida prep race for the 1977 Derby.

U nsmilingly and
unsentimentally, Bill Hartack compiled one of
the most impressive riding records in Derby
history: five wins in twelve mounts. And it's
not like they were all favorites. While
Northern Dancer was 3-1 and
Majestic Prince just 6-5, Iron Liege
paid $18.80; Venetian Way
$14.60; and Decidedly $19.40.
Decidedly and Northern Dancer
both broke the track record.

You can get a thumbnail
sketch of the Hartack persona from
one simple statement he made: "I do
not believe in defeat."

Hartack brought that tough-
as-nails attitude with him when he rode
out of the small tracks of West Virginia into
the big-time of racing. Eddie Arcaro called
him an s.o.b., and Louisville writer Mike
Barry referred to him as "Sweet William." That
stuff didn't bother Hartack, but he told the
writers in no uncertain terms, "Don't call
me Willie."

He had no use for unconstructive-
criticism, either.

After he rode Warbucks to a
thirteenth and last-place finish behind
Secretariat in 1973, Warbucks' owner
castigated Hartack for not urging the horse
through the stretch.

Replied Hartack: "I could have
whipped him into eighth, but I didn't want to
kill him."

From left, trainer Horatio Luro, jockey Bill Hartack, and commentator Chris Schenkel review Northern Dancer's 1964 Derby victory.

HINDOO
THE KENTUCKY DERBY, 1881

Upon learning about Hindoo, winner of the Kentucky Derby of 1881 and the champion runner all three years that he raced, a common response might be, "What a guy!" When Man o' War appeared in 1919, old timers compared him most to the astounding Hindoo.

Hindoo's most amazing accomplishment took place over a period of sixteen weeks in 1881. Between May 12 and September 1, the perfect bay with a little star on his forehead won eighteen consecutive races. No horse has ever won so many big races in so little time, and in all of them he emerged not merely victorious, but wholly triumphant. Overall, he won thirty of thirty-five starts.

The Spirit of the Times, the nation's racing newspaper of the nineteenth century, gave Hindoo this summation: "He lived in an age of Turf Titans. He battled with giants, yet he more than held his own."

Exterminator (*left*) and stablemate Sun Briar

EXTERMINATOR
THE KENTUCKY DERBY, 1918

The raggedy looking gelding ran one hundred races. A hundred times he raced the others, and fifty times he was the winner. Homely and nonchalant, he stood in the Winner's Circle. Including the 1918 Kentucky Derby, Exterminator won thirty-five stakes races, a record for all horses, everywhere. He hit the board a total of eighty-four times. You couldn't ask for anything more than Exterminator gave.

His name fit him like a glove, but the public gave him nicknames anyway. They called him "Old Bones." They called him "The Animated Hat Rack." They even called him "The DDT of the Turf."

He could sprint. He could win at a mile. He could run routes and carry heavy weights. If they had a race where you run all day, he would run all day, and when the sun set Exterminator would be leading them all into the darkness. He ran in three countries, at sixteen different tracks. Upon his death at age thirty in 1945, the Thoroughbred Record wrote, "They piled weight on him that would make a mule driver apologize to a mountain burro."

When he won the Kentucky Derby, it was his first start of the year as a three-year-old. He'd been purchased just ten days earlier by Willis Sharpe Kilmer as a morning workmate for his true Derby hope, favorite Sun Briar. When Sun Briar went lame, Kilmer ran Exterminator, who won and paid $61.20 for $2. He had ninety-five starts to go.

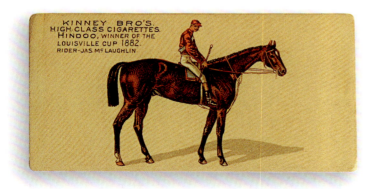

KINNEY BRO'S.
HIGH CLASS CIGARETTES.
HINDOO, WINNER OF THE
LOUISVILLE CUP 1882.
RIDER-JAS. McLAUGHLIN.

ISAAC MURPHY
THE KENTUCKY DERBY,
1884, 1890, AND 1891

T*he first inductee to the Jockey Hall of Fame, Isaac Murphy was also the first rider to win three Derbies. Murphy (third from right) was the star rider of nineteenth-century America at a time when African-American horsemen played a vital role in the sport.*

Most astonishing, Murphy won 44 percent of all races in which he rode—a feat not even approached by subsequent jockeys. Murphy was the personification of pride. He had pride in the way he rode—he was a master of pace, and hardly ever used whip or spurs—and also had pride in himself.

He was born in Lexington, Kentucky, and his original name was Isaac Burns. But his mother requested Isaac change his last name to that of his grandfather, Green Murphy, a man of solid character. All through his career, Murphy exemplified the integrity his mother hoped him to have, despite competing in an era in which betting and cheating went hand-in-hand with the shadier side of horse racing. Murphy resisted, and was honest to the bone. He once told another rider, "Just be honest and you'll have no trouble and plenty of money."

D. Wayne Lukas is the one name bigger than life in the past twenty-five years of Kentucky Derby history.

Master of the timely quote and the personification of a television sports hero, trainer Lukas has started horses eighteen straight years in the Derby, through 1998. Three won the race, and four were third. In 1996, Lukas started an incredible five horses in the Derby, which some said was overkill—but Grindstone won and Prince of Thieves ran third. The year before, he started three, with Thunder Gulch winning and Timber Country third. Timber Country won the Preakness and Thunder Gulch won the Belmont.

During a three-year span from 1994 through 1996, Lukas horses won an incredible six straight jewels in the Triple Crown. And all during that time and the decade previous, Lukas was first, or near the top, every year in money won by all North American trainers. When it comes up Derby time, a first question must be: Who has Lukas got this year?

"We've been here for a lot of years, and have a love affair with Louisville," said Lukas. "People expect us to be here."

Lukas says he feels a bit like an elder spokesman.

"Over the years, I think what has happened is you inherit a certain role. Maybe it's longevity. Maybe it's your personality. Maybe it's the nature of your horses or your clientele, you inherit this situation where you become somewhat of a spokesperson. And then if you can survive twenty years of it you become the guru, almost."

Obviously, D. Wayne Lukas is not a fellow who fell into something. He worked for it. Lukas started out as a high school basketball coach in Wisconsin. For fun, and to earn some money, he raced a few horses in local county fairs. He saw he had the knack, and soon was off to the West Coast, where he set the quarter horse racing world on fire. That game licked, he turned to thoroughbreds—and it's been gangbusters ever since.

EARL SANDE
THE KENTUCKY DERBY, 1923, 1925 AND 1930

Earl Sande notched his first two Kentucky Derby triumphs in the 1920s with Zev and Flying Ebony, and was considered the headiest rider of his time. Sande had retired by 1930, but Belair Stud owner William Woodward (on right in picture below) talked him into coming out of retirement to ride Gallant Fox.

Sande got the job done, winning not only the Derby, but the Preakness and Belmont as well. The sweep prompted the creation of the mythical title of "Triple Crown" for the three races.

Sande was famous not only for his deeds on the track but for the nifty verses written about him by nationally syndicated columnist Damon Runyon:

Green an' white at the home-stretch—
Who do you think'll win?
Who but a handy,
Guy like Sande
Kickin' that baby in!

NICK ZITO
THE KENTUCKY DERBY, 1991 AND 1994

Famous amongst modern-day Derby trainers is Nick Zito. But how could a guy born in Queens, New York, know the first thing about horses, much less win the Kentucky Derby twice?

It's not hard for Nick Zito to understand his own success. Zito captured the Derby in 1991 with Strike the Gold, and scored again in 1994 with Go for Gin. He did it with hard work.

"It's like I was born on a farm," said Zito. "It's like I was born in Kentucky. It's like I'm half horse. Because I've ate, slept, and drank this game all my life. How many people have had one job? I've had one job.

"Now, I worked in a bakery when I was twelve, and I cut bread," Zito said. "Then I was a butcher boy when I was like fourteen or fifteen. But right after that, and every day since, I worked on a racetrack."

Zito went on to become a great trainer who emotes sadness at the sight of a hurt horse, cries tears of joy after a Derby win, and testifies about his belief in angels to television viewers. These endearing eccentricities have been matched by his successes.

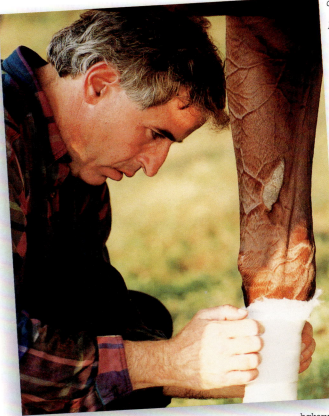

The early years of the Derby were filled with the achievements of black trainers and jockeys. Oliver Lewis won the first Derby, and Ed "Brown Dick" Brown was one of the finest trainers. But around the turn of the century, when there got to be money in racing, whites drove blacks out of the premier training and riding positions.

Caught in those changing times was a talented rider named Jimmy Winkfield, born in Chilesburg, Kentucky, not far from Lexington. Winkfield won back-to-back Derbies in 1901 and 1902, and was second and third in his only other tries. But Winkfield didn't like his ill-treatment by whites, and was the kind of guy to do something about it. He upped and moved to Russia, where he became the star rider.

But then came the Russian Revolution in 1918. Winkfield was riding in the Black Sea resort city of Odessa when he heard the cannons. He and other racetrack people grabbed a couple hundred horses and fled west into Romania and Hungary. They disguised themselves and traveled as much out of sight as possible, reaching Warsaw, Poland, after a journey of more than a thousand miles.

Winkfield then went to Paris and became a top-flight trainer. But his success there was interrupted by the Germans invading France in World War II. Once again Winkfield fled, and this time landed back in the United States. Winkfield trained in South Carolina and West Virginia for a while, then returned to France, where he trained horses into his nineties at Maisons-Laffitte.

CALUMET FARM
LEXINGTON, KENTUCKY,
1941, 1944, 1948, 1949, 1952, 1957,
1958, 1968, AND 1991

In Kentucky, Calumet Farm is more than a revered producer of nine Derby winners and numerous champion horses. There is magic in the name that conjures up the misty past. Calumet symbolizes tradition and the old-fashioned way with its fast race-horses, white wooden fences, and lush green pastures.

The farm won its first Kentucky Derby with Whirlaway in 1941 and spent more than two decades as one of the dominant forces in American racing. Calumet's fortunes declined in the 1960s, but were briefly revived with the arrival of Alydar and several filly champions in the 1970s. Eventually, the farm was sold to prominent thoroughbred sportsman Henryk deKwiatkowski, who saved the valuable land from urban development and pre-served the idyllic beauty of Calumet.

Racing fans don't think so much about the people of Calumet—of Warren Wright, who began the farm and named it after his Calumet baking powder company. They're aren't usually thinking about Wright's widow, Lucille, who married Admiral Gene Markey and carried the Calumet tradition into nostalgia. They know about that, and about trainers Ben and Jimmy Jones and jockey Eddie Arcaro. But what they really think about when they think of Calumet is a wisp of faded glory dressed in devil's red and blue.

Arcaro on Nashua

SWAPS AND NASHUA
THE KENTUCKY DERBY, 1955

Rivalries certainly create Derby heroes and often create rival bastions of fan support. In 1955, Swaps came from the West and Nashua from the East to produce one of the most talked about matchups of any Derby.

With Swaps and Nashua, the rivalry was clearly focused. Nashua, ridden by the top jock in New York, Eddie Arcaro, was the pedigreed, blue-ribbon champion of royal breeding. He was owned by multi-millionaire William Woodward, Jr., of New York, and trained by Sunny Jim Fitzsimmons. Mr. Fitz, as he was called, was bent in stature, but wise and beloved. Training for William Woodward, Sr., Mr. Fitz had won his first Kentucky Derby in 1930, with Gallant Fox, and his second with Omaha. Both those horses won the Triple Crown.

Swaps shipped from California to Louisville in a box car, and his trainer, Mesh Tenney, slept with the horse on the train and in the stall at Churchill Downs. Tenney was a cowboy coming to the urban East, and he was taking no chances. Owner Rex Ellsworth was a cowboy, too, and Swaps was ridden by the West's great jockey, Bill Shoemaker.

Swaps won the Derby, but later that summer was soundly beaten by Nashua in a match race at Washington Park, in Chicago. Which was the best? Nashua was terrific, but Swaps ended up with world records— and he won the Kentucky Derby.

Swaps (left) in training

SUNDAY SILENCE AND EASY GOER
THE KENTUCKY DERBY, 1989

It was East vs. West again in 1989 when Easy Goer, the sensation of the East, was challenged by California's Sunday Silence.

Actually, both were bred in Kentucky, but while Easy Goer was a son of mighty Alydar, born at Claiborne Farm, Sunday Silence was the son of a less fashionable stallion named Halo, and grew up across the Winchester Road from Claiborne at the Stone Farm of Arthur Hancock—the brother of Claiborne's Seth Hancock. Their father was famed horseman Bull Hancock.

One of the grandest mornings of any Derby Week came a few days before the 1989 Derby, when both Sunday Silence and Easy Goer were on the track at the same time to make their final Derby workouts. Reporters, fans, and horsepeople pressed close to the backstretch rail to see the two. Easy Goer came out and everyone gasped in admiration at the picture he made. Sunday Silence walked up to the track, tall and thin, like a high school basketball player making his way down a crowded school hallway.

Their works happened within seconds of each other, but they were a half a mile apart on the track, and people were looking both this way and that, craning their necks to see it all.

In the Derby, Sunday Silence turned on his patented burst of speed, and went on to victory, with Easy Goer closing fast, but too late.

"It was a great experience, going to the Derby with a horse of that stature," said Easy Goer's trainer Shug McGaughey. "We just got beat by a horse that could really run."

In their closest finish, Sunday Silence edged out Easy Goer at the Preakness in 1989.

BOB BAFFERT
THE KENTUCKY DERBY, 1997 AND 1998

*W*hat do you call three different horses, three different owners, three different jockeys, and just one trainer?

You could call that the Bob Baffert whirlwind, an explosion of horsepower that dominated the Kentucky Derby in 1996, '97, and '98. In Baffert's first attempt at the Derby, Cavonnier was beaten by a nose in 1996. Then the following two years Baffert won the big race with Silver Charm and Real Quiet— each horse represented by different owners and jockeys. The only constant was the white-haired, full-of-fun Baffert, who seemed to be having the time of his life while making the most of his chance of a lifetime.

"Oh, you just gotta have fun," said Baffert, who seems to have that, indeed. Before the 1998 Derby, his big horse was Indian Charlie, but he told everybody that The Fish—his nickname for Real Quiet, given because of the horse's narrow build that was more impressive from the side than front— might just come rolling by Indian Charlie in the race. "And when The Fish goes by, he'll hang out a little sign that says, 'Sorry, Charlie.'"

Baffert, a former quarter horse jockey and trainer was the top thoroughbred

trainer on the tough Southern California circuit, while grabbing a few select horses and heading east each spring to win races like the Derby and Preakness. Before the 1997 Belmont, Baffert stood at the edge of his clubhouse box and from the rail tossed Silver Charm buttons to the cheering crowd below. When Real Quiet won the Derby, Baffert's brothers fell to their knees in Baffert's path to the winners' circle to jokingly bow before Bob. And the wins go on.

How does he do it?

"I'm an ordinary Joe who caught a big wave, and I'm enjoying it," Baffert told turf writer Jay Privman.

"I went to the University of Arizona, and when I got out I decided I didn't want to work for a living, so I became a horse trainer," said Baffert.

But of course there is more to it than that.

Baffert grew up on a ranch in southern Arizona, where as the youngest kid, he was stuck with plenty of horse chores. That instinctive horsemanship shows every day at the Baffert barn, where the thoroughbreds stay sound and have long careers.

WHIRLAWAY
THE KENTUCKY DERBY, 1941

There may have been better horses than 1941 Triple Crown victor Whirlaway, but there has never been a racehorse who was livelier, more stylish, or as much fun to watch. A true American hero, he was known to his fans as "Mr. Longtail."

In many of his races before the Kentucky Derby, Whirlaway would bolt for the outside fence when the field reached the head of the stretch. But because he could run a quarter mile faster than any horse, he would often still win. A famous story recounts how, just a couple days before the Derby, trainer Ben Jones fashioned a set of blinkers that allowed Whirlaway to see primarily out of his left eye. Jones, on his pony, positioned himself just a few feet out from the rail at the end of the turn and told Arcaro to run the horse through the gap. Arcaro agreed, later saying, "I thought that if that old s.o.b. is fool enough to sit there, I'm fool enough to run him down."

Jones told Arcaro to get Whirlaway left at the gate, then make just one run. Arcaro recalled the rest of Jones' instructions.

"Once you say go, he's going to go," said Jones. "That's it, he's going to go all out. So, as late as you can keep it, do that. If you listen to me, sometime in this Derby, you'll be in front. So it's up to you when you want to be in front."

Don't forget Citation," said trainer Jimmy Jones. "He could outrun anything with hair on it."

Indeed.

Citation won at distances from five furlongs to two miles, and as Jimmy Jones' father, Ben, said, "He could catch any horse he could see."

"Big Cy" enjoyed a three-year-old season that many regard as the finest ever. He started whipping older horses early in the spring, lost a race in Maryland before the Derby, then won an astounding fifteen straight to finish the year nineteen of twenty. That included the Triple Crown and a "walkover" in the prestigious Pimlico Special, where no other horse challenged him.

Before the 1948 Derby, Ben Jones and son Jimmy had split the Calumet string, with Citation going north from Florida to Maryland with Jimmy, and Coaltown heading to Kentucky with Ben. Eddie Arcaro had his choice of the two to ride in the Derby, and was worried because some Lexington people were telling him that Coaltown's victory in the Blue Grass stamped him as the best of the two Calumet stars. According to turf writer Joe Hirsch, Arcaro asked Ben Jones to level with him. Could Coaltown beat Citation in the Kentucky Derby?

"Eddie," said Jones, "Citation can beat Coaltown doing anything."

Citation by artist Richard Stone Reeves

ROSE BLANKET
THE KENTUCKY DERBY, 1989

Beauty and roses are forever linked in the Kentucky Derby. After the official Winner's Circle ceremonies in 1989, Staci Hancock, wife of breeder and Sunday Silence part-owner Arthur Hancock, celebrated by trying on Sunday Silence's rose blanket.

The Kentucky Derby is not like any other sport. Each year about 35,000 thoroughbred horses are born, but three years later, just one *from that class will win the Kentucky Derby and make it into the glory and lasting legacy of the Winner's Circle.*

But the people who get the winning horse to the wire first are champions, too. They get to crowd their friends and family—and everyone who can claim affiliation to them at the right moment—into the Winner's Circle with them.

THE WINNER'S CIRCLE

The Kentucky Derby—and horse racing in general—is the ultimate participation sport. Besides the winning owner, trainer, jockey, groom, exercise rider, breeder, and hotwalker associated with the winning horse, there are also all the spectators who plunk down a wager on the horse who wins the Kentucky Derby. With that act of personal participation, successful bettors find their way to the Winner's Circle, too!

While it is often the names of the champion horses that can be rattled off decades after those fabled two minutes, there is a network of people who, when recalling a victory that they played some role in, bask in the glory of being a winner.

THE WINNERS
THE KENTUCKY DERBY, 1875–1998

Date	Winner	Margin	Jockey	Breeder	Owner	Trainer
May 17, 1875	Aristides	2 lengths	O. Lewis	H. Price McGrath	H. Price McGrath	Ansel Williamson
May 15, 1876	Vagrant	2 lengths	B. Swim	M. H. Sanford	William Astor	James Williams
May 22, 1877	Baden-Baden	2 lengths	W. Walker	A. J. Alexander	Daniel Swigert	Ed Brown
May 21, 1878	Day Star	1 length	J. Carter	J. M. Clay	T. J. Nichols	Lee Paul
May 20, 1879	Lord Murphy	1 length	C. Shauer	J. T. Carter	Geo. W Darden & Co.	George Rice
May 18, 1880	Fonso	7 lengths	G. Lewis	A. J. Alexander	J. S. Shawhan	Tice Hutsell
May 17, 1881	Hindoo	4 lengths	J. McLaughlin	Daniel Swigert	Dwyer Bros.	James Rowe, Sr.
May 16, 1882	Apollo	1 1/2 lengths	B. Hurd	Daniel Swigert	Morris & Patton	Green B. Morris
May 23, 1883	Leonatus	3 lengths	W. Donohue	J. Henry Miller	Chinn & Morgan	John McGinty
May 16, 1884	Buchannan	1 length	I. Murphy	Cottrill & Guest	Cottrill & Brown	William Bird

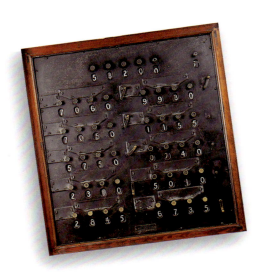

Pari-mutuel calculator

WINNING COLORS
THE KENTUCKY DERBY, 1988

*W*inning Colors graces the Winner's Circle after her 1988 Kentucky Derby victory. The gray filly became just the third of her sex to win the Derby—joining Regret (1915) and Genuine Risk (1980). Owner Eugene Klein was also the owner of the NFL San Diego Chargers, and the jockeys' silks are the same blue and gold with lightning bolt as the uniforms worn by the football team.

Date	Winner	Margin	Jockey	Breeder	Owner	Trainer
May 14, 1885	Joe Cotton	Neck	E. Henderson	A. J. Alexander	J. T. Williams	Alex Perry
May 14, 1886	Ben Ali	1/2 length	P. Duffy	Daniel Swigert	J. B. Haggin	Jim Murphy
May 11, 1887	Montrose	2 lengths	I. Lewis	Milton Young	Labold Bros.	John McGinly
May 14, 1888	Macbeth II	1 length	G. Covington	Rufus Lisle	Chicago Stable	John Campbell
May 9, 1889	Spokane	Nose	T. Kiley	Noah Armstrong	Noah Armstrong	John Rodegap
May 14, 1890	Riley	1 3/4 lengths	I. Murphy	C. H. Durkee	Edward Corrigan	Edward Corrigan
May 13, 1891	Kingman	1/2 length	I. Murphy	A. C. Franklin	Jacobin Stable	Dud Allen
May 11, 1892	Azra	Nose	A. Clayton	George J. Long	Bashford Manor	John H. Morris
May 10, 1893	Lookout	4 lengths	E. Kunze	Scoggen Bros.	Cushing & Orth	William McDaniel
May 15, 1894	Chant	6 lengths	F. Goodale	A. J. Alexander	Leigh & Rose	Eugene Leigh
May 6, 1895	Halma	5 lengths	J. Perkins	Eastin & Larrabie	Byron McClelland	Byron McClelland
May 6, 1896	Ben Brush	Nose	W. Simms	Clay & Woodford	M. F. Dwyer	Hardy Campbell
May 12, 1897	Typhoon II	Neck	F. Garner	John B. Ewing	J. C. Cahn	J. C. Cahn
May 4, 1898	Plaudit	Nose	W. Simms	Dr. J. D. Neet	John E. Madden	John E. Madden
May 4, 1899	Manuel	2 lengths	F. Taral	George J. Long	A. H. & D. H. Morris	Robert J. Walden
May 3, 1900	Lieut. Gibson	3 lengths	J. Boland	Baker & Gentry	Charles H. Smith	Charles H. Hughes
April 29, 1901	His Eminence	1 1/2 lengths	J. Winkfield	O. H. Chenault	Frank B. Van Meter	Frank B. Van Meter
May 3, 1902	Alan-a-Dale	Nose	J. Winkfield	T. C. McDowell	T. C. McDowell	T. C. McDowell
May 2, 1903	Judge Himes	3/4 length	H. Booker	Johnson N. Camden	Charles Ellison	J.P. Mayerry
May 2, 1904	Elwood	1/2 length	F. Prior	Mrs. J. B. Prather	Mrs. Charles Durnell	Charles E. Durnell
May 10, 1905	Agile	3 lengths	J. Martin	E. F. Clay	Sam S. Brown	Robert Tucker
May 2, 1906	Sir Huon	2 lengths	R. Troxler	George J. Long	George J. Long	Peter Coyne
May 6, 1907	Pink Star	2 lengths	A. Minder	J. Hal Woodford	J. Hal Woodford	W. H. Fizer
May 5, 1908	Stone Street	3 lengths	A. Pickens	J. B. Higgin	C. E. & J. W. Hamilton	John W. Hall
May 3, 1909	Wintergreen	4 lengths	V. Powers	J. B. Respess	Jerome B. Respess	Charles Mack

1877 Louisville Jockey Club membership ribbons

Willie Simms commemorative button

Date	Winner	Margin	Jockey	Breeder	Owner	Trainer
May 10, 1910	Donau	1/2 length	F. Herbert	Milton Young	William Gerst	George Ham
May 13, 1911	Meridian	3/4 length	G. Archibald	C. L. Harrison	R. F. Carman	Albert Ewing
May 11, 1912	Worth	Neck	C. H. Shilling	R. H. McCarter Potter	H. C. Hallenbeck	Frank M. Taylor
May 10, 1913	Donerail	1/2 length	R. Goose	T. P. Hayes	T. P. Hayes	T. P. Hayes
May 9, 1914	Old Rosebud	8 lengths	J. McCabe	John E. Madden	Hamilton C. Applegate	Frank D. Weir
May 8, 1915	Regret	2 lengths	J. Notter	H. P. Whitney	H. P. Whitney	James Rowe, Sr.
May 13, 1916	George Smith	Neck	J. Loftus	Chinn & Forsythe	John Sanford	Hollie Hughes
May 12, 1917	Omar Khayyam	2 lengths	C. Borel	Sir John Robinson	Billings & Johnson	C. T. Patteron
May 11, 1918	Exterminator	1 length	W. Knapp	F. D. Knight	Willis Sharpe Kilmer	Henry McDaniel
May 10, 1919	Sir Barton	5 lengths	J. Loftus	Madden & Goach	J. K. L. Ross	H. Guy Badwell
May 8, 1920	Paul Jones	Head	T. Rice	John E. Madden	Ral Parr	William Garth
May 7, 1921	Behave Yourself	Head	C. Thompson	E. R. Bradley	E. R. Bradley	H. J. Thompson
May 13, 1922	Morvich	1 1/2 lengths	A. Johnson	A. B. Spreckels	Ben Block	Fred Burlew
May 19, 1923	Zev	1 1/2 lengths	E. Sande	John E. Madden	Rancocas Stable	D. J. Leary
May 17, 1924	Black Gold	1/2 length	J. D. Mooney	Mrs. Ross M. Hoots	Mrs. Rosa M. Hoots	Hanly Webb
May 16, 1925	Flying Ebony	1 1/2 lengths	E. Sande	John E. Madden	Gifford A. Cochran	William B. Duke
May 15, 1926	Bubbling Over	5 lengths	A. Johnson	Idle Hour Stock Farm	Idle Hour Stock Farm	H. J. Thompson
May 14, 1927	Whiskery	Head	L. McAtee	H. P. Whitney	H. P. Whitney	Fred Hopkins
May 19, 1928	Reigh Count	3 lengths	C. Lang	Willis Sharpe Kilmer	Mrs. John D. Hertz	Bert S. Michell
May 18, 1929	Clyde Van Dusen	2 lengths	L. McAtee	H. P. Gardner	H. P. Gardner	Clyde Van Dusen
May 17, 1930	Gallant Fox	2 lengths	E. Sande	Belair Stud	Belair Stud	James Fitzsimmons
May 16, 1931	Twenty Grand	4 lengths	C. Kurtsinger	Greentree Stable	Greentree Stable	James Rowe, Jr.
May 7, 1932	Burgoo King	5 lengths	E. James	Idle Hour Stock Farm and H. N. Davis	E. R. Bradley	H. J. Thompson

Commemorative bracelet for July 4, 1878 match race between Ten Broeck and Mollie McCarthy

Bronze statuette of Zev

ZEV 1923

Date	Winner	Margin	Jockey	Breeder	Owner	Trainer
May 6, 1933	Brokers Tip	Nose	D. Meade	Idle Hour Stock Farm	E. R. Bradley	H. J. Thompson
May 5, 1934	Cavalcade	2 1/2 lengths	M. Garner	F. W. Armstrong	Brookmeade Stable	Robert A. Smith
May 4, 1935	Omaha	1 1/2 lengths	W. Saunders	Belair Stud	Belair Stud	James Fitzsimmons
May 2, 1936	Bold Venture	Head	I. Hanford	Morton L. Schwartz	Morton L. Schwartz	Max Hirsch
May 8, 1937	War Admiral	1 3/4 lengths	C. Kurtsinger	Samuel D. Riddle	Glen Riddle Farms	George Conway
May 7, 1938	Lawrin	1 length	E. Arcaro	Herbert Woolf	Woolford Farm	Ben A. Jones
May 6, 1939	Johnstown	8 lengths	J. Stout	A. B. Hancock	Belair Stud	James Fitzsimmons
May 4, 1940	Gallahadion	1 1/2 lengths	C. Bierman	R. A. Fairbairn	Milky Way Farms	Roy Waldron
May 3, 1941	Whirlaway	8 lengths	E. Arcaro	Calumet Farm	Calumet Farm	Ben A. Jones
May 2, 1942	Shut Out	2 1/4 lengths	W. Wright	Greentree Stable	Greentree Stable	John M. Gaver
May 1, 1943	Count Fleet	3 lengths	J. Longden	Mrs. John D. Hertz	Mrs. John D. Hertz	G. Don Cameron
May 6, 1944	Pensive	4 1/2 lengths	C. McCreary	Calumet Farm	Calumet Farm	Ben A. Jones
June 9, 1945	Hoop Jr.	6 lengths	E. Arcaro	R. A Fairbairn	Fred W. Hooper	Ivan H. Parke
May 4, 1946	Assault	8 lengths	W. Mehrtens	King Ranch	King Ranch	Max Hirsch
May 3, 1947	Jet Pilot	Head	E. Guerin	A.B. Hancock and Mrs R. A. Van Clief	Maine Chance Farm	Tom Smith
May 1, 1948	Citation	3 1/2 lengths	E. Arcaro	Calumet Farm	Calumet Farm	Ben A. Jones
May 7, 1949	Ponder	3 lengths	S. Brooks	Calumet Farm	Calumet Farm	Ben A. Jones
May 6, 1950	Middleground	1 1/4 lengths	W. Boland	King Ranch	King Ranch	Max Hirsch
May 5, 1951	Count Turf	4 lengths	C. McCreary	Dr. & Mrs. F. P.Miller	Jack J. Amiel	Sol Rutchick
May 3, 1952	Hill Gail	2 lengths	E. Arcaro	Calumet Farm	Calumet Farm	Ben A. Jones
May 2, 1953	Dark Star	Head	H. Moreno	Warner L. Jones, Jr.	Coin Hoy Stable	Eddie Hayward
May 1, 1954	Determine	1 1/2 lengths	R. York	Dr. Eslie Asbury	Andrew J. Crevolin	Willie Molter
May 7, 1955	Swaps	1 1/2 lengths	W. Shoemaker	Rex C. Ellsworth	Rex C. Ellsworth	Mesh A. Tenney
May 5, 1956	Needles	3/4 length	D. Erb	William E. Leach	D & H Stable	Hugh L. Fontaine
May 4, 1957	Iron Liege	Nose	B. Hartack	Calumet Farm	Calumet Farm	H. A. Jones

Tote board numbers

Cigarette jockey trading cards

Date	Winner	Margin	Jockey	Breeder	Owner	Trainer
May 3, 1958	Tim Tam	1/2 length	I. Valenzuela	Calumet Farm	Calumet Farm	H. A. Jones
May 2, 1959	Tomy Lee	Nose	W. Shoemaker	D. H. Wills	Mr. & Mrs. Fred. Turner, Jr.	Frank Childs
May 7, 1960	Venetian Way	3 1/2 lengths	B. Hartack	John W. Greathouse	Sunny Blue Farm	Vic J. Sovinski
May 6, 1961	Carry Back	3/4 length	J. Sellers	Jack A. Price	Mrs. Katherine Price	Jack A. Price
May 5, 1962	Decidedly	2 1/4 lengths	B. Hartack	George A. Pope, Jr	.El Peco Ranch	Horatio A. Luro
May 4, 1963	Chateaugay	11/4 lengths	B. Baeza	John W. Galbrealth'	Darby Dan Farm	Jimmy P. Conway
May 2, 1964	Northern Dancer	Neck	B. Hartack	E. P. Taylor	Windfields Farm	Horatio A. Luro
May 1, 1965	Lucky Debonair	Neck	W. Shoemaker	Danada Farm	Mrs. Ada L. Rice	Frank Calrone
May 7, 1966	Kauai King	1/2 length	D. Brumfield	Pine Brook Farm	Ford Stable	Henry Forrest
May 6, 1967	Proud Clarion	1 length	B. Ussery	John W. Galbreath'	Darby Dan Farm	Loyd Gentry
May 4, 1968	Forward Pass**	Disqualified	I. Valenzuela	Calumet Farm	Calumet Farm	Henry Forrest
May 3, 1969	Majestic Prince	Neck	B. Hartack	Leslie Combs II	Frank McMahon	John Longden
May 2, 1970	Dust Commander	5 lengths	M. Manganello	Pullen Bros.	Robert E. Lehmann	Don Combs
May 1, 1971	Canonero II	3 3/4 lengths	G. Avila	Edward B. Benjamin	Edgar Caibett	Juan Arias
May 6, 1972	Riva Ridge	3 3/4 lengths	R. Turcotte	Meadow Stud, Inc.	Meadow Stable	Lucien Laurin
May 5, 1973	Secretariat	2 1/2 lengths	R. Turcotte	Meadow Stud, Inc.	Meadow Stable	Lucien Laurin
May 4, 1974	Cannonade	2 1/4 lengths	A. Cordero, Jr.	John M. Olin	John M. Olin	Woody C. Stephens
May 3, 1975	Foolish Pleasure	1 3/4 lengths	J. Vasquez	Waldemar Farms, Inc.	John L. Greer	LeRoy Jolley
May 1, 1976	Bold Forbes	1 length	A. Cordero, Jr.	Eaton Farms & Red Bull Stable	E. R. Tizol	Laz Barrera
May 7, 1977	Seattle Slew	1 3/4 lengths	J. Cruguet	Ben S. Castleman	Karen L. Taylor	William H. Turner, Jr.
May 6, 1978	Affirmed	1 1/2 lengths	S. Cauthen	Harbor View Farm	Harbor View Farm	Laz Barrera
May 5, 1979	Spectacular Bid	2 3/4 lengths	R. Franklin	Mrs. W. M. Jason & Mrs. Wm. Gilmore	Hawksworth Farm	Grover G. (Bud) Delp
May 3, 1980	Genuine Risk	1 length	J. Vasquez	Mrs. G. W. Humphrey	Mrs B. R. Firestone	LeRoy Jolley
May 2, 1981	Pleasant Colony	3/4 length	J. Velasquez	Thomas M. Evans	Buckland Farm	John Campo

**Placed first upon disqualification of Dancer's Image*

Kentucky Derby toy truck

Date	Winner	Margin	Jockey	Breeder	Owner	Trainer
May 1, 1982	Gato Del Sol	2 1/2 lengths	E. Delahoussaye	A. Hancock III & L. Peters	A. Hancock III & L. Peters	Edwin Gregson
May 7, 1983	Sunny's Halo	2 lengths	E. Delahoussaye	David J. Foster	David J. Foster Racing Stable	David C. Cross, Jr.
May 5, 1984	Swale	3 1/4 lengths	L. Pincay, Jr.	Claiborne Farm	Claiborne Farm	Woody C. Stephens
May 4, 1985	Spend a Buck	5 3/4 lengths	A. Cordero, Jr.	Rowe Harper	Hunter Farm	Cam Gambolati
May 3, 1986	Ferdinand	2 1/4 lengths	W. Shoemaker	Howard B. Keck	Mrs. Elizabeth Keck	Charlie Whittingham
May 2, 1987	Alysheba	3/4 length	C. McCarron	Preston Madden	Dorothy/Pam Scharbauer	Jack Van Berg
May 7, 1988	Winning Colors	Neck	G. Stevens	Echo Valley Horse Farm, Inc.	Eugene V. Klein	D. Wayne Lukas
May 6, 1989	Sunday Silence	2 1/2 lengths	P. Valenzuela	Oak Cliff Thor. Ltd.	J. Hancock C. Whittingham & Dr. E. Gaillard	Charlie Whittingham
May 5, 1990	Unbridled	3 1/2 lengths	C. Perret	Tartan Farms Corp.	Mrs. Frances A. Genter	Carl Nafzger
May 4, 1991	Strike the Gold	1 3/4 lengths	C. Antley	Calumet Farm	B. Giles Brophy, Wm. J. Condren & Jos. M. Cornacchia	Nick Zito
May 2, 1992	Lil E. Tee	1 length	P. Day	Larry Littman	W. Cal Partee	Lynn Whiting
May 1, 1993	Sea Hero	2 1/2 lengths	J. Bailey	Paul Mellon	Paul Mellon	MacKenzie Miller
May 7, 1994	Go for Gin	2 lengths	C. McCarron	Pamela du Pont Darmstad	Wm. J. Condren & Jos. M. Cornacchia	Nick Zito
May 6, 1995	Thunder Gulch	2 1/4 lengths	G. Stevens	Peter M. Brant	Michael Tabor	D. Wayne Lukas
May 4, 1996	Grindstone	Nose	J. Bailey	Overbrook Farm	Overbrook Farm	D. Wayne Lukas
May 3, 1997	Silver Charm	Head	G. Stevens	Mary L. Wootton	R. and B. Lewis	Bob Baffert
May 2, 1998	Real Quiet	1/2 length	K. Desormeaux	Little Hill Farm	Michael E. Pegram	Bob Baffert

Cigarette trading cards

Pieces of Derby memories, such as these rare horseracing trading cards (left), are from the collection of the Kentucky Derby Museum. The museum honors the Kentucky Derby, its winners, and the sport of thoroughbred horse racing in America.

SIXTY FIRST

KENTUCKY

DERBY

CHURCHILL DOWNS MAY 4 1935

OFFICIAL PROGRAM ★ 10 CENTS

Lifelong racing fan Mike
Pegram jubilously lifts the Kentucky Derby
trophy on the Victory Stand at Churchill Downs
to celebrate the triumph of his horse, Real Quiet.

When Real Quiet just missed
winning the Belmont Stakes, costing the horse
the Triple Crown—and the owner a $5 million
Triple Crown Challenge bonus—Pegram
wasn't complaining.

"I've had a hell of a ride this year,"
Pegram told Knight-Ridder writer Timothy
Dwyer. "My horse is a champion. He may not
be a great horse, but he has a great heart.
Anybody who says he doesn't will get
whipped by me."

A
  ARISTIDES,
  CHURCHILL DOWNS

Aristides, first
winner of the Kentucky Derby in 1875, is
immortalized in a bronze statue in the
Churchill Downs Clubhouse Garden.

The Legacy and the Goal

As the Kentucky Derby reaches yet another milestone in its 125 years of thoroughbred racing, I find myself in the perplexing but agreeable position of simultaneous reflection and anticipation. As the country's longest-running spectator sport, the Derby has a rich and charming history that we relish reliving each spring. Yet resting on our laurels will surely prevent us from realizing the full and exciting future that such an American institution deserves. Nurturing this hybrid of tradition and innovation is what I hold to be the goal of Churchill Downs, the caretaker of the Kentucky Derby.

My enduring metaphor for the Derby is that of a magnificent painting. It is a work of art that was created a long time ago, largely through the efforts of Colonel Matt J. Winn, my predecessors, and the people who have worked with them along the way. The canvas is the Kentucky Derby. Today, our role is to protect that canvas and position it in a contemporary frame that protects the Derby and allows it to get as much visibility as possible.

We intend to preserve the essence of the Derby: the large field of the world's best three-year-old horses, the pageantry of fashion, the anticipation of witnessing the "greatest two minutes in sports," the presence of an international press corps, and the diverse congregation of people.

But the framing of the event—the responsibility of Churchill Downs—will continue to include sweeping improvements and additions to the grounds that still maintain architectural integrity as well as advancements in garnering exposure for this singular racing event.

We are currently developing a master footprint that will provide a development plan for the space and activities we hope to accommodate. Increased electronic betting, more computer-generated information available to an information-based generation, and alternative gaming options at the track will be paired with entertainment facilities such as restaurants, movie theaters, amphitheaters, and virtual reality venues to create an exciting, lively, and enduring event.

We are on the cusp of what is probably the brightest time in Churchill Downs' history. The longevity of racing clearly demonstrates that the sport is a product that people absolutely enjoy. For them, it is the thrill of it, seeing the horses run, the smells and the sounds—and most of all, the enjoyment of being a winner. We have embraced change but are determined to preserve the same atmosphere that brought a young Matt Winn and thousands of other Kentuckians out to the track 125 years ago.

—Thomas H. Meeker, President and CEO, Churchill Downs

INDEX

PHOTOGRAPHY CREDITS

SOURCE MATERIAL

Page 28: Wharton, Mary E., and Edward L. Bowen. 1980. *The Horse World of the Bluegrass.* Lexington, Kentucky: John Bradford Press. (p. 4)

Page 29: Menke, Frank G. 1945. *Down the Stretch: The Story of Colonel Matt J. Winn.* New York: Smith & Durrell. (p. 23–24)

Page 39: Chew, Peter. 1974. *The Kentucky Derby: The First 100 Years.* Boston: Houghton Mifflin Co. (p. 24)

Page 45, 47: Menke (p. 3–4)

Page 48: Reed, Billy. 1977. *Famous Kentuckians.* Louisville, Kentucky: Data Courier, Inc. (p.70–71)

Page 55: Ruby, Earl. 1974. *The Golden Goose.* Verona, Wisconsin: Edco-Vis Associates, Inc. (p. 141–142)

Page 57: Bolus, Jim. 1974. *Run for the Roses: 100 Years at the Kentucky Derby.* New York: Hawthorn Books. (p. 13)

Page 93: Bolus (p. 10–11)

Page 149: Shoemaker, Willie, and Dan Smith. 1976. *The Shoe: Willie Shoemaker's Illustrated Book of Racing.*

Chicago: Rand McNally & Company. (p. 11)

Page 151: Herbert, Kimberly S. "A Fairy Tale Come True." *The Blood-Horse.* vol. CXX, no. 18. (p. 2126-2127)

Page 154: Bolus (p. 16)

Page 156: Bolus (p. 40)

Page 157: Chew (p. 37)

Page 165: Hirsch, Joe, and Gene Plowden. 1974. *In the Winner's Circle: The Jones Boys of Calumet Farm.* New York: Mason & Lipscomb Publishers. (p. 81)